THE SALT SMART GUIDE TO PREVENTING, DIAGNOSING, AND TREATING DISEASES OF MARINE FISHES

JAY HEMDAL

Saltwater Smarts

The Salt Smart Guide to Preventing, Diagnosing, and Treating Diseases of Marine Fishes © Saltwater Smarts. All Rights Reserved, except where otherwise noted.

CONTENTS

Introduction — 1
Disclaimer — iii

1. Selecting Healthy Specimens — 4
   Fish health starts at the source — 4
   How else can you ensure new specimens are healthy? — 6
   Cyanide collection continues! — 6
   Visual inspection — 7
   Sustainability — 9
   Acclimating animals to new aquariums — 10
   Quarantine procedures — 18

2. The Importance of Accurate Diagnosis — 28
   Develop a history of your aquarium — 29
   Step-by-step problem solving — 30
   When the cure is worse than the disease — 32
   Diagnostic bath procedures — 35
   A basic fish necropsy technique — 39

3.	**Husbandry, Environment, and Your Fishes' Health**	45
	Dietary issues	45
	Water quality	56
	Dissolved gases	60
	Goiter (thyroid hyperplasia)	65
	Head and Lateral Line Erosion (HLLE)	66
	Wounds and injuries	71
4.	**Diseases of Marine Aquarium Fishes**	78
	Cryptocaryon irritans (saltwater ich, marine white spot disease)	79
	Amyloodinium (marine velvet disease)	86
	Brooklynellosis (clownfish disease)	88
	Uronema marinum (red-band syndrome)	91
	Monogenean flatworms (eye flukes, gill flukes, skin flukes)	94
	Turbellarian infection (black spot disease, black ich, tang disease)	103
	Parasitic crustaceans (copepods, isopods, and sea lice)	106
	Bacterial infections	111
	Fungal infections	115
	Internal parasites	117
	Viral diseases	122
	Exophthalmia and other eye diseases	134
	Tumors (neoplasms)	147
5.	**Diseases of Invertebrates**	150
6.	**Euthanasia**	160
	Do fish feel pain?	160

7.	Zoonosis and Dangerous Marine Organisms	164
	Zoonotic disease	161
	Preventing human infection	162
	Dangerous marine animals and plants	163
8.	Fish Pharmacology and Formulary	172
	Methods of administering chemotherapeutics	165
	Frequency of administration	166
	Drug types	167
	Formulary	173
	Closing Thought	183
	About the Author	184
	About the Publisher	185
	References	186

INTRODUCTION

Having a thriving marine aquarium in your home or office can be desirable and gratifying for a variety of possible reasons. It might serve as a constant reminder of that wonderful snorkeling or scuba-diving adventure you had in some far-flung tropical locale. Perhaps you might be inspired by the scientific aspect of aquarium keeping and the ongoing potential for acquiring knowledge or educating your kids. Or maybe you just want a source of beauty and calming tranquility to help drain some of the stress from your daily life.

Whatever your motivation for setting up a marine aquarium system, you'll quickly discover that providing proper environmental conditions is vitally important in maintaining healthy, vibrant fish. However, even the best-maintained and most naturalistic marine aquarium is still an artificial environment for fish. Try as we might to provide an ideal marine habitat, there's no getting around the fact that captivity imposes at least some degree of stress on the fish in our care—and stress can lead to disease.

At some point, every marine fishkeeper will encounter fish-health issues and must shift from being proactive (maintaining proper environmental conditions) to being reactive (treating the fish for an active disease) in their approach to care. When it's your turn to make this transition, you'll want to be armed with as much accurate information as possible so you can intervene and treat your ailing fish in a timely and effective manner.

Using straightforward, reader-friendly terminology, this guide explores the topic of fish diseases and marine aquarium medicine in a manner that will allow you, the home aquarist, the best chance of success while maximizing the lifespan of your captive animals.

This last point is important because the marine aquarium hobby is often criticized by conservationists, whether fairly or unfairly, because some aspects of the wild collection of animals are not sustainable. Keeping your fish disease-free, or treating them effectively if they do become ill, vastly reduces the number of replacement fish that are taken from the wild, making our hobby much more sustainable in turn.

So, whether you currently have a sick fish and want to identify the disease and proper course of treatment, or you simply want to be better informed about diseases you might encounter in the future, read on. You'll find that this guide is a great place to start.

DISCLAIMER

Because I cannot see your aquarium, and since aquarium fish health issues are so complex, please understand that the information provided here, while as accurate as I can make it, may not resolve the issue you're experiencing.

Any advice provided is for informational purposes only and does not constitute medical advice. The use of and access to this guide is not intended to create a veterinarian/patient relationship between you and the author. You should not rely on any information in this guide without first confirming its accuracy from other sources. You must ultimately decide whether the advice provided here is appropriate for your situation.

Medication dosages are given as examples only. Follow all product labeling and keep all medications out of the reach of children.

CHAPTER 1.

SELECTING HEALTHY SPECIMENS

The number-one goal of any marine aquarist is to have a thriving aquarium filled with healthy, long-lived animals. Achieving this goal begins with acquiring healthy fish and then handling them properly afterwards. This goal remains elusive to some aquarists, and buying sick fish is a major stumbling block, but there are steps you can take when choosing and purchasing livestock that will greatly enhance your odds of success.

FISH HEALTH STARTS AT THE SOURCE

Choosing the right source for your aquarium livestock

is a vital first step. Some fish are so damaged by the collection and transport process that no aquarist, no matter how experienced, will be able to keep them alive.

Generally speaking, captive-raised animals should be your first choice. These are relatively disease-free and already accustomed to captivity and feeding on prepared food. Additionally, over generations, captive-raised animals become domesticated and are just genetically better suited to aquarium life than wild fish are.

This blueline angelfish (*Chaetodontoplus septentrionalis*) was captive raised in southeast Asia.

The next best choice would be wild-collected fish from certified-sustainable sources. Though they're currently hard to come by, look for fish labeled with phrases such as "captive-conditioned."

Most aquarists, however, end up buying wild-collected fish from non-certified sources. This can be a very risky venture because in certain fish, the mortality rate for the first 40 days after collection can be in excess of 60%.

HOW ELSE CAN YOU ENSURE NEW SPECIMENS ARE HEALTHY?

Other steps the home aquarist can take to reduce this mortality include:

- Waiting to buy a fish until after it has been in your dealer's tanks for two weeks.
- Buying "pre-quarantined" fish (which should still be quarantined by you, however!).
- Buying fish that were collected in one of the better locations: the United States, Japan, the Red Sea, Australia, Sri Lanka, East Africa, or Fiji.

Areas where collections are suspected to be less sustainable include the Philippines, Vietnam, and Indonesia. Of course, aquarists should always avoid fish that have an unknown history, as you then have no basis for knowing how healthy they are or where they came from.

CYANIDE COLLECTION CONTINUES!

The collection of marine aquarium fishes with sodium cyanide has been well documented and is the number-one cause of death in freshly collected marine fish from certain regions. Exporters handling these fish tend to either categorically deny that this takes place or just sidestep the issue and say that it doesn't harm the fish.

In one study, 61% of a group of suspected cyanide-collected fish died within 30 days of their importation. None of the control fish in the aquarium system died, and only 9.1% of the fish originating from more sustainable areas, including Hawaii and Sri Lanka, died during the same time. The sample size was 448 fish, so it was large enough to reveal a general trend.

A similar test undertaken in 2006 showed that 55% of a group of Philippine and Indonesian fish died within 30 days of importation versus 3.1% of the control fish in the same systems. In a third study, which followed a group of marine fish for 40 days after their arrival, 55.9% of the fish from suspect areas died while only 6.2% of the fish acquired from more sustainable regions and quarantined in the same system (at the same time) died.

VISUAL INSPECTION

One of the best methods to determine whether fish are healthy is to inspect them yourself. Obviously, this precludes buying fish online or by mail-order, where you have to rely on the shipper to select good-quality fish for you.

The first step is to visit your favorite pet store and look to see what species they have in stock. Write down the names of any likely animals, and then leave without buying anything!

The next step is vital; you need to research the species you are interested in buying, both for compatibility with the rest of your animals and to determine whether you will be able to meet their needs. Once you have developed a "short list" of species you are looking for, return to the pet store and inspect the available animals for any of the following points that should disqualify them as a potential purchase:

- Signs of *Cryptocaryon* (marine ich) on ANY fish in the same water system as the one you wish to purchase.
- Cloudy appearance to the fish's skin or eyes.
- Major fin damage or missing scales.
- Rapid gill respiration rate (greater than 80 to 100 beats per minute).
- Abnormal thinness in the fish's abdomen or behind the eyes.
- Lethargy, hanging near the surface, or excessive shyness.
- Anything that just doesn't look right to you *could* be an issue. There are many more fish in the sea. Wait for a better-quality animal to come along!

If the fish passes muster to this point, ask the dealer to feed the fish a bit of food while you watch. Quality pet stores will accommodate your request. Those that won't either know the fish won't feed or simply don't want to take the time for this simple request. The fish should actively feed on food items of a type you will be able to supply. Beware of a fish that seems to be feeding but spits most of the food back out; this is a symptom of serious internal issues.

SUSTAINABILITY

All aquarists, both public and private, consume wildlife; animals are taken from the wild and are never returned. We have to ask ourselves, "Is this removal from the wild justified?"

Some environmental groups would say no, based on animal-rights issues. Others would argue that unless the collection of animals can be proven to be sustainable, it is not justifiable based on ecological concerns.

Longnose butterflyfish (*Forcipiger flavissimus*) are generally hardy and fairly disease resistant once acclimated to aquarium life.

Hobbyists know that aquarium animals can teach them, their friends, and their families much about the aquatic environment, instilling a sense of conservationism at the same time. Still, it is important to always treat your animals in a proper and humane manner so naysayers have no justification for criticism.

Consider that when hobbyists lose aquarium specimens to influences such as disease, improper environmental conditions, or tankmate aggression, it's a natural impulse to replace that deceased specimen with another one. So, every aquarium fish that survives and thrives in captivity is one less taken from the ocean.

ACCLIMATING ANIMALS TO NEW AQUARIUMS

When an animal is moved from one environment to another—such as a marine fish being transferred from a dealer's tank to a hobbyist's tank—it's often necessary for it to adapt to a different set of conditions. This process is termed acclimation.

If the two environments have very similar conditions, no acclimation is required. If, on the other hand, the differences between the source and destination environment are too great, even extensive acclimation may not be sufficient to prevent the animal from suffering stress during the transition. The key is to know what environmental differences truly matter and what degree of change can be harmful.

There is also a broader use of the term "acclimation," for example acclimating a wild animal to captivity. With respect to aquarium fish, this process begins when the specimen is first captured and doesn't conclude until it is swimming and feeding normally in the destination aquarium—a process that can take months.

THE FOUR FORMS OF STRESS

Stress in animals can take four forms:

1. Chronic stress is low-level stress that takes place over a long period. A fish that is constantly being chased by another fish is undergoing chronic stress.
2. Acute stress is more severe and takes place in a short time. A fish whose tail fin is being bitten by a tankmate multiple times per hour is undergoing acute stress.
3. Peracute stress is seen in very severe conditions that rapidly lead to death. A fish that has jumped out of an aquarium will suffer peracute stress.
4. Subclinical stress can occur over any time frame but is so minimal that there are no outward signs. Some aquarists feel that simply being in captivity leads to subclinical stress in fish and that this is a precursor to many fish diseases. However, do not lose sight of the fact that stress isn't unique to fish kept in aquariums. Fish in the wild suffer from all manner of stress, some very serious.

STRESS AND RESPIRATION RATE

Respiration rates can be a measure of overall stress; stressed fish breathe more rapidly than non-stressed ones do. In one informal study, respiration rates of wild fish were compared to similar fish in captivity, and the wild fish were found to respire faster. This was apparently due to the chronic stress they were enduring—avoiding predators, swimming against currents, etc.

HOW CRITICAL IS TEMPERATURE ACCLIMATION?

Stress experienced by fish during acclimation for temperature alone may not be nearly as important as some aquarists believe. Think about fish that regularly swim through stratified water levels (called thermoclines). Temperature swings of up to 10 degrees Fahrenheit are not uncommon, yet this is normal for these fish. Many fisheries biologists who routinely plant game fish in new waters choose not to acclimate for temperature alone unless the difference is greater than 8 degrees Fahrenheit. Changes in pH and osmotic balance (salt content) are much more important parameters that require acclimation.

A SIMPLE ACCLIMATION PROCESS

The following process is one that should be employed for all normal acclimation of animals from one system to another.

1. If possible, determine the water quality values for the aquarium that the fish will be coming from and adjust the receiving aquarium's values to a similar range. As mentioned, if the values can be made nearly identical, no acclimation process is even required.

2. The fish must be transported from one aquarium to another in a manner that minimizes additional stress. The fish should be kept in the dark, and supplemental aeration or oxygen must be used for any transport lasting longer than about 30 minutes. Heat or ice packs may be required to maintain a

proper water temperature during long transports. If you have control over it, treat the transport container carefully to avoid exposing the fish to any undue physical shock. Remember that losses during transport are always skewed to the very end of the transport time, so delays must be minimized.

3. Once at the destination aquarium, dim the room lights and float the sealed bag in the aquarium for 10 to 15 minutes. This is sufficient to equalize the water temperatures.

4. If you don't already know the values, check the pH and specific gravity of the aquarium and the shipping water. Long-duration shipments (greater than 24 hours) need to be handled differently and are described below. Avoid any increases in specific gravity greater than .004 units—adjust the receiving tank's specific gravity to match that in the transport bag.

5. Open the bag, and roll the top in on itself to form a floatation collar. Remove as much of the shipping water as you can while still keeping the fish in an adequate volume of water. Add to the bag a volume of aquarium water that equals **25%** of the volume of water in the bag. (For example, if the bag holds 8 ounces of water, you would add 2 ounces of tank water.) The fish is now 20% equilibrated. Wait five minutes.

6. Remove enough water from the bag to reduce it to its starting volume, and now add a volume of tank

water that equals **50%** of the volume in the bag. Wait another five minutes.

7. Remove water from the bag a third time, again reducing it to the starting volume, then add a volume of tank water that equals **100%** of the water in the bag (the bag is now 75% equilibrated). Wait five minutes.

8. Release the specimen into the tank. Most aquarists avoid letting any of the acclimation water enter their tank. If the animal has been released into a tank housing other fish, monitor them very closely for signs of compatibility problems.

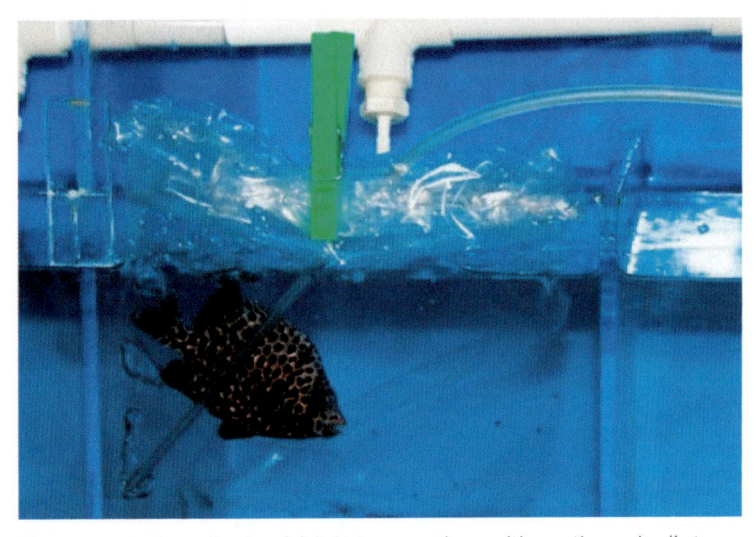

The proper way to acclimate a fish in its transport bag—with aeration and a clip to hold the bag secure.

BEGIN THE QUARANTINE PHASE

The next three days serve as a period of adaptation for the new fish. You should offer it various foods and evaluate it daily to ensure it is maintaining body weight and that its behavior is normal. It often helps to measure the fish's respiration rate and be aware of any changes.

Experienced aquarists can just look at a fish and see whether it is respiring too rapidly, but if you are unfamiliar with what is "normal," it helps to actually count the gill beats in 15 seconds and then multiply that by four to get gill beats per minute. This measurement can be taken daily, and any rise of, perhaps, 20% should be a matter of concern. As a baseline, most small tropical marine fish respire at a rate of less than 100 BPM.

FLOW (DRIP) ACCLIMATION

Some advanced aquarists and fish importers utilize a technique known as "drip acclimation," where a small hose is set up to siphon water from the main aquarium into an acclimation container. Home aquarists often try to emulate this method but almost always set the water flow rate too low. For example, for one liter of water, if the drip line is set to one drop of water per second, it would take 50 hours to reach 90% equilibrium.

A rate of flow of one milliliter per second will result in one liter of shipping water reaching 90% equilibration in 2½ hours, a much more reasonable time frame. Even then, the aquarist must supply supplemental aeration and possibly heating during the time.

The proper way to drip-acclimate fish (cover removed for clarity).

SPECIAL CASES

Not every acclimation can be handled by the simple method described above. The following are special cases that may require aquarists to deviate from the regular procedure:

- During the winter, a shipment of fish may arrive severely chilled. Remove the bags from the shipping box, and then remove any outer plastic bags or paper wrappings and lay the bags in the room in dim light. Do not float the bags in the aquarium yet, as this will reduce proper gas exchange. After 30 minutes or so, the fish's shipping water will have warmed up a bit and the simple acclimation procedure can begin.

- Sometimes, bags are punctured during shipment, and some invertebrates are shipped "damp." In these cases, no acclimation is possible. Just place the animal directly into the aquarium.

- Any animal that arrives moribund (not moving or upside-down in the shipping bag) is undergoing peracute stress. Eliminating this takes precedence over trying to minimize the perceived acute stress of not acclimating the animal properly. Adding the fish directly to the aquarium as in step 2 is actually the best course of action. Some fish that arrive barely breathing can actually be revived by holding their mouth open into a gentle current to help ventilate their gill chambers.

- Starfish, sea urchins, octopuses, and some crustaceans are extremely sensitive to changes in pH and specific gravity.

- Marine fish do not tolerate significant increases in specific gravity. If the difference is .003 or greater, consider lowering the specific gravity of the receiving aquarium to more closely match that of the shipping water. On the other hand, fish handle reductions in specific gravity very well. Fish can be moved from high to low specific gravity through the normal acclimation process, even if the change is as great as .006 specific gravity units.

Acclimation is an important technique and is a necessary first step when introducing fish to a new aquarium. The most common mistake seen is when people begin to think, "If acclimation is so important, then a really long acclimation time must be even better." Stick to reasonable acclimation rates, and your fish will respond well—and they'll thank you by thriving in their new home.

QUARANTINE PROCEDURES

All too often, aquarists buy a new, seemingly healthy fish and add it to their main display tank, only to watch a major disease epidemic occur in the aquarium less than two weeks later. Did the new fish bring the disease into the aquarium? Did the added stress of the new fish in the environment simply allow an existing latent disease to become deadly? Was it simply pure bad luck? Regardless of the reason, the aquarist is now faced with a disease problem in his or her aquarium.

All new fish must be assumed to be harboring disease, regardless of their history. Freshly captured wild fish, fish from pet shops, as well as locally tank-raised fish can potentially transmit infections to a stable aquarium population (aside from causing mortality in the new fish themselves).

Scrawled filefish (*Aluterus scriptus*) often develop a number of rarely seen diseases when held in captivity.

To help control these problems, all new fish should undergo a quarantine procedure prior to their introduction into an aquarium housing other fish. These quarantine protocols often represent a compromise between their degree of effectiveness, the level of effort required, and the safety of the animals themselves.

At one end of the spectrum is using no quarantine procedure at all, which is the easiest course of action but obviously the least effective. At the other end is a very comprehensive quarantine protocol that can require months to perform and utilizes a wide variety of medications along with veterinary services to determine that the fish are free of all disease. A middle-ground approach is best for the home aquarist. Using simple visual symptoms from the fish combined with uncomplicated but effective prophylactic treatments, new fish can be more safely added to an established aquarium.

Eels, such as this dragon moray (*Enchelycore pardalis*), are resistant to many common fish diseases.

GENERAL FISH QUARANTINE

The following process works well in most cases, with minimal risk to the new fish, but always be prepared to modify the process if circumstances require it.

Active quarantine begins after the preliminary quarantine phase described in the previous section. The actual quarantine procedure used is determined by the type of fish being processed and the resources at the aquarist's disposal.

Remember that many diseases can be transmitted on wet surfaces and as droplets through the air, so it's important to disinfect tank tools that are used in more than one system—or use a dedicated set of tools for each system—and to avoid locating quarantine tanks close to your main aquarium.

Step 1 – The quarantine system must be established before acquiring any new fish. Many aquarists find it helpful to establish a biological filter in their main aquarium a month or so before transferring it over for use in the quarantine system. Sponge filters and canister filters work very well for this purpose. If the water quality in your main aquarium is good, you can use water removed from it during water changes to fill your quarantine tank. These techniques make the assumption, of course, that your main aquarium is operating disease-free.

A basic quarantine system consists of an aquarium large enough to temporarily house any fish you expect to acquire, a tank cover, aeration, a heater, a biofilter, and some inert hiding places, such as pieces of PVC pipe. Do not use any calcium-based materials, as these will interfere with copper treatments if they're needed.

Also, the true volume of the quarantine tank needs to be determined. This is often less than an aquarium's advertised volume (or it could be more if there is a sump attached to the system). The most accurate means to determine the volume of an aquarium system is to measure the amount of water it takes to fill the total system, with all decorations in place, up to its normal water level. If that is not possible, the aquarium volume can be calculated (as described in the formulary section).

Step 2 – Begin an anti-protozoan treatment. The three

options for this include organic copper, ionic copper, and chloroquine. Most beginning and intermediate aquarists should choose the organic copper option. Public aquariums often use the ionic copper method, while advanced aquarists have been experimenting with using chloroquine for this stage.

Organically chelated copper quarantine:

There are a variety of copper medications on the market that contain copper chelated (bound) to an organic chemical. This makes the copper less toxic to the fish and more stable in solution. Basically, you add the medication once and then add more only if partial water changes are made.

One drawback to these medications is that they work fairly slowly and may not eradicate an active disease in time to save all the fish. Another drawback is their proprietary nature; manufacturers do not disclose how they are made, so it is difficult to choose one brand over another. Use your dealer's advice to select a product to use. Finally, they work best as a preventative and, like ionic copper, cannot be used with invertebrates present.

Organic copper is added to the aquarium for a treatment length of at least 30 days. Because step three needs to begin sooner than that, the praziquantel treatment it entails will need to be run concurrently.

Ionic copper sulfate quarantine:

This method requires a source of ionic copper and a good-quality copper test kit. The copper concentration is slowly raised to between .18 and .21 ppm ionic copper and maintained at this concentration for 14 days. No chemical filtration should be used during this treatment (including carbon and ion-exchange resins). The copper level should be checked twice daily and partial doses added to maintain the proper concentration at all times. Be aware that if the aquarium has been exposed to an organically chelated copper medication in the past, any residual copper will interfere with the ionic copper test.

During the treatment, watch the fish closely for signs of copper toxicity. Unfortunately, these signs are almost identical to the symptoms of many protozoan diseases (scratching, rapid breathing, pale coloration, copious mucus production, cloudy eyes and fins), so care must be taken to ensure that copper toxicity is actually the problem. Sharks, rays, mandarinfish, pygmy angelfish, seahorses, and jawfish are among some of the species known to be sensitive to copper levels as low as .15 ppm. Invertebrates have differing sensitivity to copper, but most species cannot tolerate copper ion concentrations above .025 ppm.

Bicolor angelfish (*Centropyge bicolor*) are sensitive to copper treatments.

At the conclusion of the treatment, the copper concentration can be allowed to drop on its own or you can remove it via chemical filtration or partial water changes.

Chloroquine quarantine:

Chloroquine is reportedly used at a wide range of concentrations, from 5 to 20 milligrams per liter (mg/l). This huge range is likely a result of too few studies being performed to determine the best dosage.

The 5 mg/l dose should be used as a quarantine preventative (not for active diseases) or for treating delicate species (although little is known about the sensitivity of different fish species to this medication). A dose of 8 mg/l is considered the "standard dose" for treating most active protozoan infections, while the 20 mg/l dose would be reserved for attempting to eradicate difficult-to-treat *Uronema marinum* infections. Toxicity in some fish species has been reported at doses above 15 mg/l. Wrasses, surgeonfish, and lionfish seem to be very sensitive to chloroquine. The length of a typical chloroquine treatment is 14 days (as a preventative) to 30 days (for an active infection).

Chloroquine is also toxic to many invertebrates, algae, and bacteria. Seriously high ammonia levels (greater than 1 mg/l NH3-N) are sometimes seen a few days to a week after dosing an aquarium with chloroquine. It is unknown why this is seen in some aquariums but not others. One hypothesis is that the chloroquine has a direct antibiotic effect on the nitrifying bacteria. Another idea is that the chloroquine kills so much microscopic life in the aquarium that the beneficial bacteria are overwhelmed and an ammonia spike develops. Most likely, the cause is a combination of both factors. Always monitor the ammonia levels in aquariums during treatment with chloroquine.

Step 3 – Begin a treatment for metazoan (multi-celled) parasites, in this case various worms. These infections are very common but take longer to cause fish loss, so anti-protozoan treatments are administered first. The worm treatment of choice is praziquantel. The typical treatment is to dose it at 2.2 mg/l, then after 72 hours, change 50% of the water, re-dose, and wait another 72 hours.

Praziquantel is not very soluble in water, so it needs to be mixed by hand. Wearing rubber gloves and a dust mask, place the proper amount of praziquantel into a brine shrimp net and partially submerge the net in the aquarium. Gently knead the net so the fine particles of the drug drift out into the aquarium. Continue the process until you have expressed all of it into the water. Then invert the net and give it a final rinse in the aquarium water. There are proprietary formulations of praziquantel on the market that may be easier to dose than the pure powder, but the resulting drug concentration may not be easily determined.

Another possible worm treatment is the "dip-and-move" method. Fish are given a 166 mg/l formalin dip for 45 minutes and then moved to a new aquarium for 24 to 48 hours. This process is then repeated as many times as practical. Using two tanks that are cleaned out between uses, this process can be repeated many times. A minimum of six moves is suggested.

Step 4 – At the end of any quarantine procedure, the fish should be observed for a minimum of 14 days prior to moving them to an aquarium containing established animals. During this time, the fish should be watched for other possible problems, such as bacterial diseases, internal parasites, etc. Suitable treatments should follow the positive identification of any of these other problems.

There should never be a rush to place specimens into a main aquarium at the conclusion of a quarantine procedure. These methods are not infallible, and a delay after the conclusion of the procedure acts as a safety net to allow any remaining diseases time to develop and be treated outside the main system. Quarantining new fish is time consuming and expensive, but it is well worth the effort in terms of overall lower mortality in your fishes.

Special note: "Observational quarantine" is a term you might hear. It involves a technique that is used when one wishes not to expose a new specimen to any procedure more drastic than environmental control and observation pending the development of any obvious disease symptoms. The use of this technique should be limited to extremely delicate fish, such as flashlight fish, or fish that do not normally transfer diseases to bony fishes, such as sharks and rays.

The specimen is placed into an isolation tank and observed for signs of disease for a period of 30 days. The difference between this technique and no quarantine at all is that the problem of disease transfer is minimized on a case-by-case basis in choosing "low-risk" or "low-value" tankmates. In addition, the operative word *observational* is very important. At least twice daily, the animal must be inspected closely for signs of developing problems. However, don't make the mistake of relying on observational quarantine simply because it is easier because there are certainly more effective techniques.

CHAPTER 2.

THE IMPORTANCE OF ACCURATE DIAGNOSIS

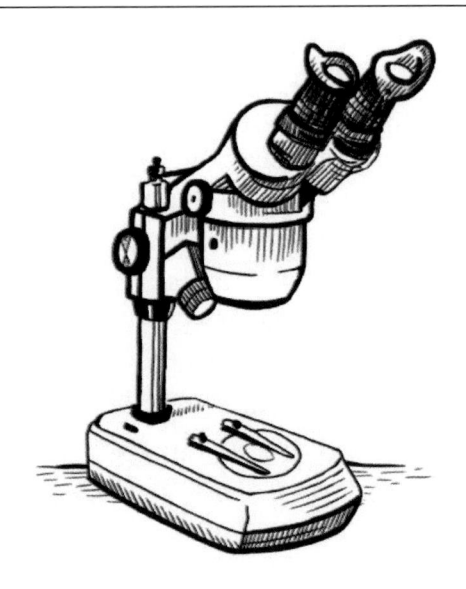

Determining the best course of action for any problem with your aquarium can be a difficult task, and the diagnosis and treatment of a fish disease is no exception. Even advanced aquarists will often need to seek the help of others for such complicated issues.

Online resources, such as forums, are available, but they have two major drawbacks. First, the people responding to your question may not be experienced enough to offer a viable solution. Second, more than one solution may be offered, making it difficult to determine which course of treatment to follow.

As a public aquarium curator with many years of experience in the husbandry of fish and invertebrates, my goal here is to offer expert, authoritative advice on how to address your fish-disease issues. But before we can get to that, you have a little problem-solving to do on your own.

DEVELOP A HISTORY OF YOUR AQUARIUM

When you go to your doctor with a medical complaint, the first thing he or she will do is ask for your health history—any current problems you're having, specific symptoms you've been experiencing, health issues you've had in the past, medications you're taking, your lifestyle habits, etc. Well, solving a fish-disease problem is much the same. The more complete the information you can compile about the problem, the easier it will be to find the right solution.

Applying any of the advice in this guide will require that you first know the following information about your aquarium:

AQUARIUM PARAMETERS

- Aquarium water volume (actual volume)
- Filtration type
- Lighting

WATER QUALITY

- Temperature
- pH
- Salinity
- Ammonia
- Nitrite
- Nitrate

IN-DEPTH INFORMATION

- Have you lost any fish to this problem yet? Once this has happened, it is difficult to stop a disease problem fast enough to prevent additional fish losses.
- What is the respiration rate of the affected fish (count this in gill beats per minute)?
- Are the affected fish still feeding?
- What solutions have you tried so far?

STEP-BY-STEP PROBLEM SOLVING

The following five steps outline a process that will help home aquarists recognize and react to animal health problems in their aquariums sooner rather than later:

Step 1 – Recognize that there actually is a problem. If something looks just a little bit "off" with a fish, there is almost always a much more serious underlying problem. As exotic animal veterinarian Mark Loyd once said, "Beware of any animal that suddenly presents itself as 'ADR.'" That acronym, he explained in a Southern drawl, simply stands for "Ain't Doin' Right." This phrase describes that mildly unsettling feeling you get when you observe an animal and notice that something appears to be different but you can't really be sure there even is a problem.

The main danger with an "ADR" case is in doing nothing because the problem seems to be so insignificant. In reality, you may need to react very quickly. With aquatic animals, sometimes the only timely clues you get are very subtle changes in behavior. The passage of less than 24 hours from the start of symptoms to an untreated animal's death is not unheard of.

Step 2 – Identify the potential solutions. Once the problem is identified, research the various solutions. List all possibilities: Your fish have tail rot; do you then just cut their fins off? Your fish keep dying; so do you change your hobby to stamp collecting? These may not be your primary solutions, but list them anyway, along with (hopefully) more suitable alternatives!

Step 3 – Select the solution(s). The simplest answer is often your best initial choice. Rank all the potential solutions in descending order of practicality, risk to the animal, and the potential for success so that you will have a secondary plan of action ready in the event that your first solution fails to solve the problem.

Step 4 – Implement the solution. Once you've done this, give it a fair chance to work. For example, many antibiotics do not show much effectiveness until they have been used for four to seven days. Changing the type of antibiotic used prior to that time may mean that you have skipped over a potential cure for the problem.

Step 5 – Record the results. Whether just for your personal records or for passing the information onto other aquarists, it is vitally important to record the results of this process. Success or failure, if you do not record your results, the opportunity to share the information with others is lost.

And remember, those who don't learn from history are doomed to repeat it! Long-term aquarists with bad memories (like me) will find that if they do not keep good records, they will inevitably waste time working out solutions to problems they originally solved many years ago.

WHEN THE CURE IS WORSE THAN THE DISEASE

With some fish diseases, a proposed cure may actually be more damaging than the illness itself. In human medicine, this is called the iatrogenic effect, where the proposed cure causes its own serious problems. To avoid this, aquarists must always be aware of the Latin phrase *"Primum non nocere,"* or "First, do no harm."

Problems in developing an appropriate disease treatment can range from treating an aquarium with a medication or dosage that ends up being lethal to the fish to procrastinating due to indecision, again with fish loss as a result. In between these two extremes are using products that simply do not work as advertised, treating for the wrong disease, or trying too many different treatments.

DOUBLE CHECK THE DOSAGE AND STOCK UP

Always double check your dosage calculations before adding any medication to an aquarium. Some medications can be toxic to sensitive species, notably ionic copper and chloroquine. Also, aquarists may well want to stock up on certain common medications, as it is very disheartening to diagnose a serious disease in your aquarium only to find the stores are closed. Never ignore early symptoms with the thought that "maybe the fish will get better on its own," as this almost never happens.

BUYER BEWARE!

When it comes to aquarium medications, another Latin phrase to remember is *"Caveat emptor"*—"Let the buyer beware." It's unfortunate, but there is little control over the aquarium medication manufacturers. People can develop "cures" and sell them as effective treatments without ever having to prove that their product is safe or even works at all.

Also, beware of most "reef-safe" medications. There is strong pressure from hobbyists for the market to develop medications that are safe to use with sensitive invertebrates. To fill this need, products are made and sold, but most have not been tested for effectiveness.

The red spider sponge (*Trikentrion flabelliforme*), actually a red sponge with a white zoanthid growing on it, is very sensitive to aquarium medications.

TREAT FOR THE RIGHT DISEASE

Treating for an incorrect diagnosis is another common issue. Many diseases have symptoms that mimic each other and overlap. Aquarists may conclude that their fish has one disease, when it actually has another.

GIVE THE TREATMENT TIME

Finally, "hunting and pecking" is seen when a desperate aquarist tries a treatment and, when it doesn't seem to be working, switches to another and then another. The trouble is that many fish medications take five to seven days, or even longer, to work. You have to give them an appropriate amount of time to do their job.

DIAGNOSTIC BATH PROCEDURES

Aquarists often do not have at their disposal sophisticated tools for diagnosing diseases. As a result, acute diseases are sometimes treated based solely on gross visual symptoms. At other times, fish may be chronically infested with parasites, but because they may initially show few if any symptoms, a treatment regimen is not enacted as rapidly as it might be.

One tool to aid aquarists in the prompt identification of metazoan and protozoan parasites is the "diagnostic dip" or "bath." In this procedure, the fish to be examined is placed in a solution designed to cause the parasites to become dislodged from the host's skin or gills. This solution is then settled to concentrate any pathogens for microscopic observation. If parasites are discovered during the course of this procedure, an effective treatment can then begin based on the proper identification of the disease. Should the procedure not reveal parasites, the aquarist may then wish to focus his or her attention on other possible causes.

STEP-BY-STEP DIAGNOSTIC BATH

Here are the procedures that should be followed when performing a diagnostic bath:

Step 1 – The specimen must first be evaluated with the following questions in mind:

- Are there valid reasons for attempting this potentially stressful procedure (is the fish newly acquired, showing obvious disease symptoms, etc.)?

- Can the specimen be removed from the tank for evaluation?
- Does this species of fish have a known intolerance to formalin solutions?
- What is the minimum size container that will safely house the animal during the procedure?

Step 2 – Fill a container (one that is inert in water and has a flat, smooth bottom is best) with an appropriate amount of aquarium water. To exclude particulate matter that may be in suspension in the tank, it may be helpful to pre-filter this water (a 53-micron plankton sieve will do the job). Add formalin (37% formaldehyde gas in an aqueous solution) at a rate of 13 drops per gallon (166 ppm). Specimens housed in water cooler than 68 degrees Fahrenheit (20 degrees Celsius) may require a slightly higher concentration of formalin. Place the container so that it is elevated off the floor, and use an airstone so the solution will be properly aerated during the procedure.

Step 3 – Fill a second container (at least as large as the first one) with water from the aquarium. Capture the fish in a non-abrasive net, and rinse it in this second container for a few moments. This will wash away most of the extraneous matter from the fish's skin that may have accumulated during the capture procedure. This material, detritus and algae filaments, would otherwise make the final examination of the dip water more difficult. Gently place the fish in the formalin/water solution, and cover the container to keep the fish secure and calm. Begin timing the procedure now.

Step 4 – Observe the fish at 5-minute intervals for evidence of stress. Should any major indication of stress be noted (loss of equilibrium, improper breathing rate, etc.), the procedure may need to be terminated early. After one hour, return the fish to the aquarium, remove the airstone from the dip solution, and incline the container at a 20- to 35-degree angle from horizontal.

Step 5 – After the bath solution has settled for 30 minutes, siphon a portion of the water from the bottom of the container (especially the lowest point) into a smaller glass container. Some surface water may also need to be collected if there is any indication of fish mucus floating at the surface. Another means of concentrating the sample is to then pour the remaining sample through a plankton sieve and gently wash the material captured by the sieve into the smaller container. Generally, collecting a volume of 5 to 10% of the original in this manner is sufficient. Repeat the process with the concentrated sample (inclining the container, settling for 30 minutes, siphoning off 5 to 10%) until the volume of the sample is of an appropriate size for the planned microscopic examination (50 mL is suitable). Any parasites that have become dislodged from the skin and gills of the fish should now be concentrated in a small volume of water.

A centrifuge (if you have access to one) may be used to further concentrate the sample. Be sure to use this at low speed to avoid distorting the morphology of the parasites, which would make identification more difficult.

Step 6 – Properly dispose of all unused bath solution,

and begin the microscopic examination promptly. Using the final concentrated solution, examine a portion of the sample under a low-power dissecting microscope for evidence of metazoan parasites. It is often advantageous to repeat this inspection with a different sub-sample to ensure that nothing is missed. Next, place a few drops of the sample under a compound microscope at 60 to 100 power and check for the presence of protozoans. If the sample is agitated during the removal of these portions, allow time for the sample to resettle.

INTERPRETING THE RESULTS

Interpreting the results of a diagnostic bath requires some experience in that the parasites may have been changed morphologically by exposure to the formalin. Worms may have become contorted by the dip, but look for eyespots, hooks, or suckers. Crustacean parasites are more easily identified. The only difficulty is making sure that the crustacean seen is actually a parasite and not some free-living, harmless species. Generally, the presence of any parasitic metazoan indicates the need for a treatment regimen to be initiated, but any incidental, non-parasitic protozoans that may be present do not necessarily indicate the need for treatment.

OSMOTIC DIFFERENTIAL BATHS

Formalin is not the only irritant that can be used to dislodge parasites during a diagnostic bath. Osmotic differential baths (exposing a marine fish to fresh water, and vice versa) are also effective at loosening parasites. However, there is a greater possibility that the shape of the organism will be disrupted by osmotic pressure to such an extent that proper identification would be difficult.

SKIN SCRAPE VS. DIAGNOSTIC BATH

Biopsies, or "skin scrapes," are often performed on live specimens as a similar diagnostic tool to the bath procedure. You can acquire a sample faster by performing a biopsy, but the stress to the animal is greater due to the physical abrasion that occurs. A biopsy, promptly examined, has the benefit over the bath procedure of collecting live parasites—and the motion of a living protozoan parasite makes microscopic identification much easier.

On the other hand, one major advantage of the diagnostic dip is that a formalin bath is oftentimes the prescribed treatment for the very pathogens that the bath is used to identify. This means that should a problem be discovered during the course of the procedure, the diagnostic bath itself will have already had some therapeutic effect.

A BASIC FISH NECROPSY TECHNIQUE

Whenever any aquarium animal dies, the first question that inevitably arises is "why?" In some cases, as in a fish that jumped from the aquarium, the answer is immediately obvious. In other instances, the cause of death cannot be determined with even the most extensive necropsy (autopsy) procedure. Between these two extremes lies the necropsy procedure outlined below.

While not every hobbyist will have the wherewithal or willingness to perform a necropsy, this method, if performed properly, can often determine the cause of death attributed to all external protozoans, metazoans, and fungal infections, as well as most internal metazoan and some bacterial infections and environmental problems. It is deficient in identifying the cause of death from viral agents and most bacterial infections. Nutritional disorders can sometimes be noted but rarely attributed to a specific factor.

A SOLID SUCCESS RATE

Still, out of 571 necropsies performed over the past 11 years (none taking longer than 30 minutes to perform), there was shown to be a definitive cause of death in 43% of the cases. In these instances, necropsies were not performed on specimens for which the cause of death was evident by cursory examination (tankmate aggression, escaping a tank, *Cryptocaryon*, etc.), so a 43% success rate is very good since it included only the tougher cases.

In terms of results, these necropsies can be broken down as follows:

Environmental (shipping trauma, ammonia, etc.)	20%
Protozoan (ciliates, flagellates, all single-celled parasites)	9%
Metazoan (multi-cellular parasites, worms, and crustaceans)	7%
Bacterial (visual identification of *Mycobacterium*)	5%
Fungal (external species such as *Saprolegnea*)	2%
Viral (lymphocystis)	<1%

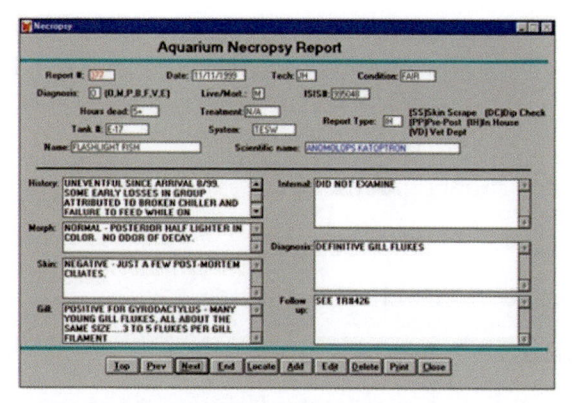

The above figure is an example of a necropsy records database and shows some of the important information that should be recorded about fish that have undergone a necropsy. This format could easily be converted to a paper log format if desired. This process is important; there is little point in taking the time to go through the necropsy procedure if the information gathered will not be available to you at a later date, and you can't rely on memory to keep detailed records.

The most important facet of a successful necropsy using this method is the condition of the specimen to be examined. The fresher the sample, the better the results. Specimens that have been frozen prior to examination are useless; the tissues will have changed too drastically. Furthermore, any fish that has been dead long enough for decomposition to have set in will be much more difficult to examine.

The science of invertebrate necropsy is still in its infancy, so the following method can be applied to fish only.

WHAT YOU'LL NEED

In addition to a fresh specimen, the aquarist will need the following minimal amount of tools (optional items are marked with an asterisk):

- Dissecting microscope (to identify metazoans, fungus, and most protozoans)
- Dissecting kit
- Latex rubber gloves
- Dissecting tray
- Sterile fresh and marine water
- Slides and cover slips
- *Compound microscope (for smaller protozoans and some bacteria)
- *Scale and calipers
- *Specimen jars and 10% buffered formalin solution (to preserve samples)

This procedure progresses in a linear fashion from an initial cursory assessment, to more involved examinations, to (hopefully) an accurate diagnosis. The process shouldn't stop there—the final step is the follow-up, a treatment or some other resolution so that additional fish do not die in the same fashion. After each point in the procedure, determine whether a diagnosis can be made; if not, proceed to the next step.

THE NECROPSY PROCEDURE

1. Determine the fish's history. Was it recently moved to a new aquarium? Had it been eating well? Had it been exposed to any other fish that subsequently died?
2. Examine the exterior of the fish by eye from all angles. Look for damaged fins, emaciation,

exophthalmia, and any other grossly visible signs. Optionally, weigh and measure the fish.

3. Using a scalpel, scrape the body of the fish from head to tail and place the resulting mucus on a slide with a drop of sterile fresh or salt water and cover with a slip. Examine under a dissecting microscope at 30x to 80x magnification.

    If the fish is freshly dead, the presence of any moving organisms should be suspect. However, fish that have been lying on the bottom of a tank for more than 30 minutes often pick up a whole collection of non-parasitic scavengers that were not actually involved with the animal's death. The basic types of parasites seen will be protozoans or metazoans, in some cases both. If the mucus is devoid of life, try a second scrape just to confirm the first negative result.

4. Perform the same technique using a clip from the fish's gills. Are the gill filaments filled with red blood cells or are they pale (which might indicate anemia or is an artifact of the fish having been dead for too long)?

    Optionally, examine a thin section of gill under an oil immersion lens. In some cases, bacterial gill disease can be confirmed without staining or culturing—but the organisms are right at the limit of visibility.

    In the case of the gills, any damage or the presence of living organisms should be considered highly suspect as the cause of death. Gills are a vital organ and are rich in blood for parasites to feed on. Furthermore, scavengers do not reach the gill chamber of a dead fish too easily, so the presence of incidental post-mortem organisms is less likely.

5. Using a sharp scalpel, open the fish's body cavity from the anal opening through the gill arch, and cut back the body wall on one side to expose the internal organs.

   Remove the stomach and intestine, and open them up. Look for the presence/absence of food and place samples under a dissecting scope as in step #3 to look for parasites.

   Grossly examine the other organs—look for white or yellow nodules in the liver or spleen. Make a wet-mount slide of any nodules located. Look for protozoan cysts. In the absence of this, the nodules may very well be a symptom of a *Mycobacterium* sp. bacterial infection.

6. The necropsy procedure using the equipment outlined above usually stops at this point. Further examination requires histopathology techniques performed by a laboratory. Always dispose of animal waste and used glass slides in a safe manner, and always wear gloves when performing these procedures.

CHAPTER 3.

HUSBANDRY, ENVIRONMENT, AND YOUR FISHES' HEALTH

Health problems that develop in fish aren't always a simple matter of otherwise robust specimens being exposed to pathogens or parasites. In many cases, there's an underlying husbandry or environmental issue that either impacts the fish's health directly or weakens the specimen's immune system, rendering it more vulnerable to disease-causing organisms. Among these factors are:

DIETARY ISSUES

Proper nutrition is vital to all animals. The fish in your

aquarium rely solely on you to meet all of their dietary requirements, and their food must be provided in sufficient quantity to supply the energy they need in order to grow. The diet must also have the proper balance of fats, proteins, and carbohydrates, as well as the proper amount of vitamins and minerals.

On the other hand, too much food or food that is too high in calories will cause the fish to become obese. Not all fish have the same dietary requirements, and their needs even change as they grow. To top it off, over-feeding an aquarium can result in deteriorating water quality that will harm the fish.

Other dietary issues aquarium hobbyists may encounter in their fish include:

NUTRITIONAL DISEASES

Good nutrition is important in maintaining a basic level of disease resistance in fish, but remember that diet alone is not the only factor that can induce or prevent diseases in fish. Most dietary/nutritional diseases are chronic in nature, taking long periods to develop. Diagnosis is difficult, and secondary infections may actually end up being the primary cause of death, even though it was perhaps an inadequate diet that left the animal susceptible to the infection in the first place.

AMINO ACID DEFICIENCY

This condition is not very common and usually must be demonstrated in the lab by feeding specific amino-acid-deficient foods. A lack of the essential amino acid tryptophan causes reversible scoliosis. In other cases, anemia or poor growth may be the only symptoms.

FOOD POISONING

Though this problem is rarely identified, it's important to avoid feeding poor-quality, rancid foods to fish, as doing so can cause acute problems. For example, aflatoxin from contaminated grain (cottonseed) feeds can cause liver cell carcinoma (hepatoma) with a very high rate of incidence (greater than 57%) in trout having been fed contaminated foods.

NUTRITIONAL DEFICIENCIES

The following table lists various vitamins and nutrients, as well as the symptoms that may appear in fish when they are lacking. Notice that many of the symptoms of vitamin deficiency are rather vague, easily confused with other disease problems and, in some cases, very similar to each other.

Water-soluble vitamins	Symptoms
Ascorbic acid	Scoliosis, altered cartilage, possibly lateral line erosion
B12	Poor growth, fragile red blood cells
Biotin	Skin lesions, poor growth, and fragile red blood cells
Choline	Fatty liver, poor food conversion, kidney disease
Folic acid	Lethargy, poor growth, dark coloration
Inositol	Poor growth, distended gut
Niacin	Loss of appetite, muscle spasms, skin lesions
Pantothenic acid	Gill hyperplasia, poor appetite and growth
Riboflavin	Eye problems, cloudy lenses, etc.
Thiamin	Edema, poor growth, convulsions
Fat-soluble vitamins	
Vitamin A	Retinal alterations, poor growth
Vitamin E	Muscular dystrophy, edema, poor growth
Vitamin K	Blood clotting problems
Other nutrients	
Essential fatty acids	Poor growth, eventual death
Fiber	Constipation, buoyancy problems
Iodine	Goiter
Protein	Poor growth rate

FATTY LIVER DISEASE

A major chronic health problem facing most long-term captive marine fishes is "fatty liver disease," or liver degeneration. Fish do not assimilate fats well, so oftentimes, if a fish's diet is too high in fat, it will then be deposited in various tissues, especially the liver. Unlike with mammals, this fat is not readily usable during times of starvation. Even if food is withheld from a fat-laden fish, very little of the fat is ever reconverted into usable energy. Some fish do not show outward signs of obesity, especially sedentary species such as grouper. In these fish, fatty liver disease may only be diagnosed after death, when sections of the liver will show oil droplets and pieces of the liver itself will float in sea water.

Fatty liver disease is most common in adult fish whose growth rate has slowed considerably. Younger fish tend to grow fast enough to minimize fat deposition—excess calories are turned into muscle tissue instead. With long-term captive marine fish, fatty liver disease is the leading cause of (or contributor to) death. Virtually every lionfish held in captivity longer than three years will show evidence of fatty liver disease upon necropsy.

What techniques are available to solve this problem? Nothing can be done for a fish once fatty liver disease has become evident. Prevention is the only course of action an aquarist can take. Simply putting the fish on a "diet" may not work, in that this may result in increased aggression towards other fish in the aquarium. The best solution is:

- Avoid feeding herbivores diets high in meat proteins.
- Train carnivores to feed on low-protein, low-fat diets, such as squid or gelatin diet.
- Avoid feeding any saturated fats to fish. Overall

dietary fat levels should be less than 20% in actively growing fish and less than 12% in adult fish.

There has also been a theory that feeding freshwater fish to predatory marine fish will cause malnutrition and fatty liver disease. Most of the rationale behind this has to do with slightly different fat profiles between marine and freshwater prey fish species. Credence is given to the theory when so many marine aquarists report that they lost their lionfish to liver degeneration after feeding them live freshwater goldfish. In reality, they would have run into the same trouble had they fed any single fish species as a diet for their lionfish. Feeding carnivores too frequently can also cause fatty liver disease. The general recommendation is to feed larger carnivores only twice a week.

ANOREXIA

At some point, most aquarists will have a fish that refuses to feed in captivity. Once this symptom begins with a particular specimen, the "clock starts ticking." If the issue is not resolved within an appropriate period, the fish will die.

Acute anorexia (where a fish suddenly stops feeding, or never starts feeding, and soon dies) is usually caused by some environmental issue, such as water quality problems, disease, transport stress, or tankmate aggression. A rarer problem is chronic anorexia, where the fish has apparently adapted well to captivity in all respects except that it does not show a normal feeding response.

The term anorexia is replaced with inanition (loss of energy due to lack of food) or inappetance (lack of appetite) by some authors. However, the term anorexia is perhaps a better fit, as it is defined as "an aversion to food due to serious psychological problems."

In some cases, a fish that had been feeding well stops for some unknown reason. In other cases, a newly acquired fish refuses to feed despite its apparent environmental needs being met. Weight loss may or may not be apparent in the animal, and inanition is not observed until just before the fish succumbs to the long-term problem.

Some fish may go without food for extended periods and subsequently recover. These are usually older, larger fish or those kept in temperate (cool) waters. At the other extreme, a post-larval butterflyfish may succumb if it goes even a few days without food.

This dragon moray refused all food for months when first acquired from Japan. It subsequently began feeding normally.

There is a preferred course of action one should take to try to get a chronically anorexic fish to begin feeding. After the environmental problems mentioned above have all been ruled out, the second, most obvious step is to make certain that the food being offered is of a type and size known to be accepted by that species of fish. If the captive diet of the fish is unknown, or if the species is known to be a difficult feeder, the problem may not be just with the one specimen, but rather with the entire species.

Assuming that other specimens of the same type are known to feed well on the food being offered, the next step is to change the delivery method. For predatory fish, stick feeding will sometimes work to get the fish feeding normally. Simply put, a food item is impaled on the end of a long stick and offered to the fish. However, there is an art to this delivery method.

First, different species react in diverse ways to the presence of the feeding stick. Some fish ignore the stick, while others seem to shy away from even the thinnest, least visible of sticks. When in doubt, opt for a clear or very thin feeding stick. It seems that the end of the stick closest to the animal causes the most problems. Using a short length of heavy monofilament fishing line at the end of the stick helps make it less visible to the fish. Avoid wire or other overly stiff material, as the fish may strike at the food but then back away when it touches that material.

The tube-feeding process can be employed to give the fish food energy during the time it is anorexic. In some cases, this gives the aquarist enough time to determine a permanent solution. This process uses simple equipment—a syringe and a flexible plastic tube. Feline urinary catheters or avian tracheal tubes can be used for small fishes. Larger fishes can be fed using standard airline tubing attached to a large syringe. A Luer-lock syringe will hold the feeding tube more securely to the syringe body. Placing the tube is easier if you first bevel the end of it. The tube should have marks on it at regular intervals so you can more easily judge the depth of insertion.

The basic food recipe is to create a liquid that will easily pass through the feeding syringe and tube but is thick enough to carry a high amount of calories to the animal's digestive tract with the least amount of water. It is best to prepare this slurry in a blender, using components of the fish's normal diet.

The amount of food administered at one feeding is generally 2 to 4% of the animal's body weight, just enough food to cause a slight distension of the animal's belly. In most cases, the use of an anesthetic, such as MS-222, is required to sedate the fish so the tube can be inserted.

Holding the fish on its back, gently insert the tube into its mouth and try to locate the esophagus. If you are too far to one side or the other, the tube will miss and emerge from under one of the gill covers. Once in place, gentle pressure on the syringe plunger will move the liquid food into the fish's stomach. Once fed, the tube is gently withdrawn and the fish is moved to a recovery tank.

Spontaneous regurgitation is the most commonly seen problem with this method, though there are also reports of people accidentally rupturing the fish's digestive tract. Like any medical procedure, there are subtle techniques for this process that need to be learned through practice—so please do not expect to read this basic introduction and suddenly be proficient at tube-feeding fish.

Some adult scorpionfish may refuse non-living food when first acquired and will need to be trained to accept prepared food items.

Force-feeding is a technique that can be employed on larger carnivorous fishes. A sedated fish is held on its back while its mouth is opened, and a food item of appropriate size for the animal is then placed in the back of the animal's throat. A finger or semi-rigid tube is then used to gently push the food item into the stomach. In some species, such as anglerfish and eels, there are back-curved vomerine teeth in the throat that will actually grasp the food item and keep the fish from voluntarily regurgitating it.

Be cautious in directly handling a fish during either of these two techniques, as some have very sharp teeth and, of course, some fish have venomous spines.

FOOD HANDLING

Also, keep in mind these important points when handling fish foods:

- Frozen and fresh seafoods have been found to contain *Mycobacterium marinum* and other "non-pulmonary" *Mycobacterium* spp. Always wear gloves when handling aquarium food items.
- Eating, drinking, or storage of food for human use should not take place in the same immediate area as animal food preparation. Separate sections in the human food refrigerator should be made available. Do not use kitchen items used in the preparation of animal diets for human foods.
- Air thawing should be used only if the food temperature can be closely monitored and the food is refrigerated as soon as it has softened up—food sitting at room temperature after it has completely thawed is subject to bacterial contamination. This is particularly true in the summer months when room temperatures are elevated.
- Due to problems with a milky residue in frozen small krill and brine shrimp, a light tap water rinse

prior to feeding would be acceptable in order to reduce organic loading in the aquarium.
- Remember, the quality of frozen food degrades over time. After a batch of food has been stored in a household freezer (not a deep freeze) for 6 to 12 months, the quality has degraded to a point where it should be used with caution or perhaps discarded.

WATER QUALITY

Like diet, good water quality in an aquarium boosts your fishes' resistance to disease, but just to a point. Poor water quality can induce disease in fish, but in some cases, fish will become infected despite being kept in what we would consider optimum water quality. Key to maintaining good water quality is a monitoring program that will identify issues before they become serious by identifying trends.

An aquarist's water-quality-monitoring program should incorporate a variety of testing equipment to monitor all critical parameters in the water systems. The monitoring frequency varies depending on the parameter and the aquarium being tested. Aquarists are urged to keep a written log of their aquarium's water-quality data so that emerging trends can be identified and the past history of the tank will be known.

TEMPERATURE

This is the most critical, yet easiest measured water-quality parameter in most aquariums (dissolved oxygen is more critical but much more difficult to measure). The temperature parameter has the greatest potential to change rapidly due to life support (heater or chiller) malfunction.

Aquarium systems can be heated, chilled, or held at ambient temperature, and temperatures can be measured using a variety of methods. Digital electronic thermometers and infrared remote-sensing thermometers that have been calibrated using a standardized laboratory thermometer are the most "high-tech" approach. Temperature should be monitored throughout the day; automatic "out-of-range" alert systems are very handy, especially at night.

PH

This water-quality parameter, though less changeable than water temperature, gives the aquarist the most information about the overall quality of a system's water. This parameter should be measured weekly on most aquariums using a pH probe with automatic temperature calibration. Highly critical systems, such as some reef aquariums, will require a full-time pH probe to constantly monitor this parameter. The ideal pH range for marine livestock is between 8.2 and 8.4.

An aquarium's current pH level can be used to determine the potential need for a water change. As important as the actual pH value, one must also monitor the ΔpH (change in pH). If a system's pH is low but steady, no corrective action may be needed, but a system with a widely fluctuating pH, though perhaps having a relatively high average value, may be in more need of attention.

AMMONIA

Bony fishes produce ammonia as their primary waste product. If ammonia levels become elevated in an aquarium due to a non-functioning biological filter, fish loss may occur. The toxicity of ammonia is dependent on the pH and temperature of the aquarium's water. At a high pH and a high temperature (typical of marine aquariums), most of the ammonia is present in the toxic form. At lower pH levels (below 7.0) and at lower temperatures, most of the ammonia is present in the ammonium form, which is not toxic to fish.

NITRITE

Nitrite is produced by bacteria when they consume ammonia as an energy source. Although toxic to fish, sodium chloride dissolved in the aquarium water renders it less toxic. Since marine aquarium salt is about 70% sodium chloride, nitrite toxicity is rarely an issue with marine fishes.

NITRATE-NITROGEN

This parameter measures the buildup of one specific waste product resulting from the biological filtration process. While not overtly toxic itself, the absence of nitrate-nitrogen is a good indication that the water system does not correspondingly have a buildup of other, more harmful waste products, such as phenols, cresols, etc. Aquarists should perform enough routine water changes so that the nitrate ion level is always diluted below dangerous levels.

SALINITY/SPECIFIC GRAVITY

The salt content of marine aquariums should be monitored weekly, or as needed, using either a specific gravity meter or a temperature-corrected refractometer. Both of these devices should be standardized to a glass laboratory grade hydrometer. Marine fish-only systems are typically kept at a specific gravity of 1.019 to 1.022, while marine invertebrate systems are kept at a higher specific gravity of 1.023 to 1.026.

A refractometer is a good way to measure salinity and specific gravity in marine aquariums.

DISSOLVED OXYGEN

Photometric dissolved oxygen testing meters are the easiest and most practical oxygen-measuring device for pet stores and home aquarists. Dissolved oxygen meters require frequent calibration and replacement of electrode membranes, and reagent oxygen tests are difficult to perform.

As the level of dissolved oxygen is generally a function of the filtration/aeration system used and the system's bioload, it rarely changes unless one of those criteria changes, so this test is usually only performed on an as-needed basis. Dissolved oxygen readings can sometimes be used to infer total dissolved gasses, a way to help avoid supersaturation of aquarium water with air.

NON-ROUTINE PARAMETERS

Other water-quality parameters may be measured on an "as-needed" basis. Phosphorus (as orthophosphate) is best measured using a spectrophotometer; again, visual reagent tests are not accurate enough at low detection levels.

Copper is used as a medication for marine protozoan diseases, and its proper use at low concentrations requires the use of a spectrophotometer. This is a case where improperly analyzing a visual reagent test can lead to fish death.

Dissolved calcium is important for the growth of live coral and is best measured using a reagent test kit. Iodine and strontium test kits are available, but are extremely difficult to read accurately, leaving their results in doubt.

DISSOLVED GASES

All aquarists are aware that their aquariums require a minimum concentration of dissolved oxygen in the water for their fish to survive. Many aquarists are also aware that if gases are dissolved in too great an amount, supersaturation can occur, causing serious health problems in their animals. Due to a lack of appropriate test equipment, most home aquarists can do little about measuring for potential problems with dissolved gas levels.

There are four basic concerns regarding the level of dissolved gases in aquarium water: acute supersaturation, chronic supersaturation, low dissolved oxygen tension, and high carbon dioxide tension. Even without test kits and expensive meters, aquarists can avoid problems with these concerns if they are made aware of the issues and take certain precautions.

ACUTE SUPERSATURATION

This is known as the "gas bubble disease." An aquarium that has a water pump malfunction of some sort may develop a dissolved gas saturation level of greater than 120%. The onset is sudden and the results devastating. Fish will develop severe bilateral exophthalmia (pop-eye involving both eyes), and their gills will show massive trauma with aneurysms. In the worst cases, air bubbles will be present in the soft fin rays and in the gills. Death is rapid, and even if the still-living fish are moved to a new aquarium, they will usually not recover.

Two common causes of acute supersaturation are a sump that is allowed to run dry, allowing the pump to suck in air, or a loose fitting that allows for a continuous air leak at the suction side of a pump. Despite best intentions, equipment sometimes does fail, allowing supersaturation to occur.

In these cases, the problem can be lessened by always having the return line from any aquarium pump return water to the aquarium above the water line. The agitation of the pumped water hitting the aquarium surface is akin to shaking up a can of soda pop and driving off the "fizz."

Not every case of gas buildup in animal tissue is caused by supersaturation. Some bacteria produce gasses as they grow and multiply. A fish with a serious bacterial infection may develop gas pockets in the intestines, behind the eyes, in the air bladder, or even under the skin.

CHRONIC SUPERSATURATION

Only a few aquarists have ever identified this relatively rare, bizarre syndrome. Essentially, this disorder occurs when the level of supersaturation is not great enough to kill the fish outright, but sufficient to cause physical damage to the fish. It is a great mimic of other problems. For example, the damage caused by the supersaturation may be invisible to the aquarist, but it weakens the fish. In turn, the fish may develop protozoan infections or may die from a pre-existing chronic problem, such as fatty liver disease.

Since mechanical failure of a pump rarely occurs in a "partial fashion" (that is to say, only a tiny leak develops), this problem is rarely the cause of chronic supersaturation. The primary cause of this malady is the use of very cold tap water (even if subsequently warmed up) to perform partial water changes. During the winter at northern latitudes, the temperature of the tap water may fall to 38 degrees Fahrenheit. At this low temperature, water can hold a huge amount of dissolved gas. In addition, the city water supply may use powerful pumps that force even more gas into solution. When this water is used by unsuspecting aquarists, the result is chronic supersaturation (or even acute supersaturation in severe cases).

One answer to this problem is to warm up the tap water to 85 degrees Fahrenheit (30 degrees Celsius) and aerate it heavily for 48 hours prior to using it for a water change in an aquarium.

The following are symptoms of chronic supersaturation in fishes:

- Mostly smaller fish are affected (they have a higher surface-to-volume ratio).
- White "mask" on nape of head.
- Mild exophthalmia, sometimes only involving one eye.
- Discoloration of posterior soft fin rays.
- Missing scales, fin damage (resulting from aggression from the less affected fish).
- Fish loss attributed to other chronic problems, such as fatty liver disease.
- Gill aneurysms, some macroscopic air bubbles may be seen.
- Rapid, deep breathing.
- Listlessness, hanging near the surface or on the bottom.

Generally, these symptoms abate only gradually once the source of the supersaturation has been eliminated. In some instances, fish mortality continues for weeks after the incident has been resolved.

LOW DISSOLVED OXYGEN TENSION

This is the relatively common "gasping fish syndrome," in which the dissolved oxygen level of the water drops below that required by the fish. The fish will be seen breathing rapidly and deeply, often gasping at the surface. As the problem progresses, the fish may die, often with an unmistakable "last-gasp"—their mouth being fixed wide open.

Common causes of this problem include overcrowding, insufficient aeration, chemical removal of oxygen (such as by potassium permanganate), and low saturation levels due to high water temperature and high biological oxygen demand from microorganisms in the aquarium.

Generally, if the affected fish are moved to a new system that has sufficient levels of dissolved oxygen (or if the problem is quickly corrected in the original aquarium), the fish will recover spontaneously with no long-term effects. Be aware, however, that bacterial, protozoan, and metazoan gill diseases can cause similar symptoms.

HIGH CARBON DIOXIDE TENSION

In this rather rare instance, the dissolved oxygen level may be at or near saturation, but artificially elevated carbon dioxide levels create symptoms in the fish that mirror those of oxygen deficiency. There is only one situation in which a marine aquarist is likely to see this problem: in a heavily stocked aquarium that has powerheads or canister filters whose effluents do not actively break the surface tension of the water. Breaking the surface tension allows the excess carbon dioxide to be driven off.

GOITER (THYROID HYPERPLASIA)

Goiter, also called thyroid hyperplasia, develops in fishes when the thyroid tissue begins to grow outside of its normal location underneath the gills of the fish, forming a bulging protrusion.

CAUSE

A goiter can be caused by a lack of iodine in the food or water, or by substances called goitrogens, which are toxic and cause goiters to form in fish exposed to them.
With sharks and rays, high nitrate levels (greater than 30 mg/l NO_3-N) inhibit the ability of the thyroid gland to utilize available iodine. This, in turn, disrupts the thyroid gland, causing a goiter in those fish.

TREATMENT

Potassium iodide additions to the water will rarely resolve goiter in fishes. Aquarists have also tried adding elemental iodine (Lugol's solution) as well as L-thyroxine to the water, but this rarely cures the problem either.

Administering oral doses of potassium iodide (KI) directly in the animal's diet is the best way to reduce goiter in fishes. The trouble is that the dose is very small: 2.5 mg of KI per pound of animal weight, placed into a favorite food item. Potassium iodide is also very bitter, so it must be placed inside an empty gelatin capsule or the fish may taste it and reject the food.

This treatment may need to be repeated every 18 months or whenever symptoms of goiter return. Fish that have had a large goiter for a long time will be permanently affected. Also, goiters in such fish can become malignant, generally transforming into a carcinoma, which is untreatable.

Goiter protruding from the gill of an old wife fish.

HEAD AND LATERAL LINE EROSION (HLLE)

Head and Lateral Line Erosion (HLLE) is the name for a type of skin erosion that affects some species of marine fishes in captivity. It is also occasionally referred to as Marine Head and Lateral Line Erosion (MHLLE) or Head and Lateral Line Erosion Syndrome (HLLES). A similar syndrome occurs in freshwater fishes, but the causes seem to be different and it is usually termed "Hole-in-the-Head" disease.

SYMPTOMS

HLLE typically begins as small, pale pits around the fish's eyes. These may develop into light-colored lesions along the fish's lateral line system, finally spreading onto wider areas of the body and sometimes involving the unpaired fins. Fish that develop severe lesions are usually permanently disfigured. In yellow tangs, HLLE tends to cause more fin damage and less skin erosion.

HLLE in an ocean surgeonfish caused by the use of activated carbon.

VULNERABLE FISH

At least 20 families of fish have been identified as having developed HLLE in captivity (see the susceptible marine families in the table below). Not all species of fish show the same symptoms or develop lesions to the same degree. HLLE is not normally seen in fish in the wild, but some cases have been reported.

Family	Common name
Acanthuridae	Surgeonfishes
Blenniidae	Combtooth blennies
Chaetodontidae	Butterflyfishes
Gadidae	Cods
Grammatidae	Basslets and grammas
Haemulidae	Grunts
Labridae	Wrasses
Lutjanidae	Snappers
Muraenidae	Moray eels
Percichthyidae	Temperate perches
Percidae	Perches
Plesiopidae	Roundheads
Pomacanthidae	Angelfishes
Pomacentridae	Damselfishes
Scorpaenidae	Scorpionfishes
Serranidae	Sea basses and soapfishes

THE ACTIVATED CARBON CONNECTION

A relationship between the use of activated carbon in aquariums and the development of HLLE in surgeonfish has been positively shown in two scientific studies. Other than that, no formal studies have been undertaken that identify other causes. However, a multitude of unproven causes have been presented by various people. Commonly, stray electrical currents and vitamin deficiencies are cited as causes, but one of the studies mentioned above ruled these out as common causes.

Based on those preliminary observations, the Toledo Zoo

performed a study that demonstrated that, indeed, lignite carbon causes HLLE in surgeonfish. Minor HLLE lesions were noted on two study fish 20 days after the lignite carbon was added to the sump of their system. The lesions began to develop on the additional fish in that system and grew in size until after four months, all of the fish in that system showed severe lesions (eventually involving over one-third of their body surface). The control fish did not develop any lesions.

Statistically, the results were definitive that activated carbon use caused HLLE in the study fish. This is a severe case, involving the body and fins.

THE CARBON STUDY HYPOTHESIS

The basic hypothesis of this study was that activated carbon causes HLLE in fishes. Originally, it was thought that carbon dust (known as fines) was the causative agent. This was based on observations at the Toledo Zoo where carbon was removed from an aquarium and the water was changed, yet HLLE symptoms could still be produced by adding susceptible fish to the aquarium, indicating there was some unknown residual action by the carbon.

Carbon fines were frequently discovered in the filter sumps and substrate of these tanks. Changing all of the aquarium's water, decorations, and substrate would then render the aquarium safe for housing susceptible fishes (assuming no new carbon use).

Two public aquariums have reported acute outbreaks of HLLE in systems where carbon had been accidentally ground up and ejected into aquariums by mechanical filtration systems. It has also been reported that aquariums that use protein skimmers (foam fractionators) do not seem to develop HLLE as frequently, even when carbon is routinely used. Since protein skimmers remove particulate organic carbon from water (including carbon fines), it was thought that this might be the reason these systems do not cause HLLE as readily.

In addition, the hard-pelleted carbon used in this study did not cause severe HLLE, while the soft, dusty carbon did. However, no carbon fines were seen during histological examinations of the lesions of the study fish. This means either that the dust causing the effect is fleeting, the fines were too small for the histologist to see, or there is some other factor associated with carbon use that causes HLLE in susceptible fishes.

CARBON RECOMMENDATIONS

The recommendation based on the clear effect that the use of carbon had on the study fish is not to use activated lignite carbon in marine aquariums housing fish species susceptible to HLLE. Other means of water quality management should first be explored, including water changes, non-carbon chemical filtration, or protein skimming. Extruded pelleted carbon may be more suitable, especially if used sparingly. No conclusions can be drawn regarding the use of carbon filtration products that were not tested.

If you do use carbon, rinse it well in reverse osmosis water prior to use, use a protein skimmer, and do not place the carbon in a high-water-flow reactor (that might serve to break the carbon granules up into finer particles).

Yellow tangs with HLLE show different symptoms: more fin damage and less skin erosion.

WOUNDS AND INJURIES

Injuries caused by tankmate aggression or capture and transport are a common environmental issue seen in marine aquarium fishes. There are even cases of self-inflicted injuries, such as a fish jumping out of the tank (which is likely the number-one, most easily preventable cause of death with aquarium fish!).

With every injury, there are two hurdles the fish must overcome: surviving the initial injury itself (sometimes the tissue damage is so great that the fish dies from lack of blood) and fending off any secondary bacterial infection that may take place where the tissue was damaged.

TANKMATE AGGRESSION

This is a potential issue in any marine aquarium that houses more than one fish. In the most serious instances, where the aquarist severely underestimates the ability of one fish to injure another, aggression actually takes the form of predation. There are also cases of fish living peacefully side by side for years and suddenly beginning to fight.

This blacktip reef shark (*Carcharhinus melanopterus*) was slashed by a tankmate. Although it looks serious, the wound healed completely in just a few weeks.

Home aquarists are often in denial that any aggression is taking place because, with the exception of the most severe cases, it is very difficult to "catch them in the act." Take, for example, a case of minor aggression where one fish is "tagging" another one (damaging a fin with a bite) at a rate of once or twice a day. What are the chances that an aquarist is going to see the aggressive act? It is over in a split second.

Although beautiful, passer angelfish (*Holacanthus passer*) are very aggressive towards some other species.

Additionally, while you are watching your fish for signs of problems, they are busy watching you and will often suspend any overtly aggressive behavior until you leave them alone again. Left unchecked, even this seemingly minor aggression problem will cause fish loss, as the damaged fins cannot regrow fast enough and the damage mounts.

If you see ripped and torn fins on one of your fish and the number of injuries is increasing, it is best to isolate that fish either by moving it to a new aquarium or by utilizing a tank divider. Some aquarists have experimented with moving the aggressor (if it can be identified) as a sort of "time out," but this usually offers only a temporary solution to the problem.

A floating basket can serve as a temporary means to isolate fish that are fighting.

Less frequently seen are instances of "displaced aggression." In this case, a community of aquarium fish is cohabitating fine, with no aggression, but suddenly one fish turns on a tankmate with no warning and attacks it. More than just a "pecking order" or an "uneasy truce" that exists among animals in many aquariums, this is a serious problem with a rapid onset. What causes this displaced aggression? Not all fish will show this behavior, but its cause is stress imposed on one fish that is "diffused" by that fish then attacking another.

In public aquariums, the common stressor is external—e.g., a child pounding on the exhibit glass may suddenly cause an angelfish to turn and attack a damselfish. Moving tank decorations around or cleaning an aquarium may instigate displaced aggression. Red Sea fish of many species are well known to behave in this fashion, as are some temperate Australian species. In some cases, there is a cascade effect, with the attacked fish in turn attacking another and so on.

SELF-INFLICTED INJURIES

Fish occasionally do injure themselves. A frightened fish may jump out of the tank onto the floor, or an aggressive feeder may damage its mouth going after a food item. There is a saying that, "Any fish will jump out of an aquarium under some circumstances, and some fish will jump out of an aquarium under any circumstances." The corollary to this is, "The chance of this happening is always directly proportional to the value of the animal."

This dwarf bass was such an aggressive feeder that it dislocated its jaw going after food. This fish partially recovered on its own, but always had a slight jaw deformity after the event.

Most fish are "blind leapers" and just jump from their aquarium in a random direction. A simple top will keep these fish in their place. Other fish jump with more objectivity—aiming for any gap in the aquarium lid. Examples include firefish, royal grammas, and jawfish. These species require especially close-fitting tops. Still other creatures, such as octopus and eels, are "slitherers" and will actually squeeze through an opening or push a lid aside. These creatures need a close-fitting, weighted lid to keep them at home. There is also surprisingly wide variation among some families of fish; most clownfish do not jump out, but the wide-banded clownfish, *Amphiprion latezonatus*, is a well-known leaper.

CAPTURE/TRANSPORT INJURIES

Fish are sometimes injured during capture and transport. These issues should be clearly evident when you are at the pet store picking out the fish, so with practice, you should be able to avoid most of these issues. Beware of *Uronema* infections, as these are often mistaken for injuries but are actually caused by a protozoan.

TREATMENT

The standard treatment for an injured fish is to:

- Isolate it to prevent further damage.
- Keep it under dim illumination to reduce stress.
- Lower the specific gravity of the aquarium's water to around 1.018 to reduce osmotic stress that the fish may be experiencing due to its damaged skin.

If no signs of secondary bacterial infection are seen (including worsening damage after the event or redness or white growths over the wounds), then nothing more can be done. If a secondary bacterial infection begins, then antibiotic therapy may be required.

CHAPTER 4.

DISEASES OF MARINE AQUARIUM FISHES

When disease arises, you must act decisively to save the affected fish. But you can't take effective action if you don't know exactly what disease you're dealing with. This chapter takes a detailed look at the various disease-causing pathogens and pests that marine aquarium hobbyists may encounter in their fishkeeping career. Each section examines the cause and symptoms of the disease, the means of diagnosis, the prognosis for the affected fish, appropriate treatment methods, and preventive measures.

CRYPTOCARYON IRRITANS (SALTWATER ICH, MARINE WHITE SPOT DISEASE)

CAUSE

Cryptocaryon irritans, better known as saltwater ich or marine white spot disease, is a very common ciliate protozoan that every marine aquarist encounters at some point and is probably the second most common reason people leave the hobby (the first being unexplained fish loss). Capable of killing fish within 14 to 21 days, *C. irritans* causes the needless loss of many aquarium fish each year due to delays in starting treatment and/or choosing the wrong medication. Handled properly in a timely manner, ich should never cause fish loss.

SUSCEPTIBILITY VARIES

Not all species of fish are infected by *Cryptocaryon* to the same degree. Sharks and rays seem to be immune, and moray eels rarely contract it. However, powder blue and Achilles tangs (*Acanthurus leucosternon* and *Acanthurus achilles* respectively) are so prone to developing ich, that many aquarists simply avoid buying them.

LIFE CYCLE

The life cycle of this parasite is fairly straightforward:

- The stage that attaches to the skin of the fish is known as the trophont.
- After feeding on the fish's tissue for some time, the trophont drops off and becomes a tomont that exists in the substrate.

- The tomont begins to divide and releases tiny, free-swimming tomites (also called theronts). One tomont can produce about 250 tomites.

- The free-swimming tomites seek out a fish to attach to. Once they find and attach to a host fish, they mature into trophonts. It is this stage that causes problems in aquariums.

- The life cycle takes around six days at tropical temperatures. This could result in one parasite becoming 15 million in just three weeks. Because not all tomites are successful in finding a host fish, the parasite typically increases at a rate of about 10 times per week.

PROPAGULE PRESSURE AND RESISTANCE

The ease with which *Cryptocaryon* infections proceed in an aquarium is influenced by both propagule pressure and resistance. The term "propagule pressure" simply refers to the number of tomites present. If the propagule pressure is low, there are relatively few tomites present and the chances of them landing on a suitable host are very low. Thus, the infection does not reach the exponential growth phase.

Although not scientifically proven, it appears that fish that have survived a *Cryptocaryon* infection develop some resistance and are less likely to develop the disease in the future. On the other hand, a fish that is in poor overall health, or has suffered an environmental stress, may have a lowered resistance and will be more likely to develop the disease.

Remember, however, that propagule pressure is itself the most common stressor that lowers a fish's resistance to this disease. That is, if there are hundreds of tomites swarming around an aquarium, even the least-stressed fish will become infected.

SYMPTOMS

As one of its common names implies, the very first symptom of *Cryptocaryon* is the appearance of tiny white dots, about the size of a grain of table salt, on the skin and fins of just one or two of the fish in the aquarium. Beginning aquarists often miss this early symptom or mistake it for air bubbles.

At this point, the life cycle of the parasites is "in sync." That is, they tend to drop off and form tomonts at the same time, giving aquarists false hope that the fish have "cured themselves" or, worse yet, that an incorrect treatment is actually working. Typically, four to six days later, many more white spots suddenly reappear on the fish. Then, the parasites begin to become out of sync with one another and the fish begins to carry the white spots (trophonts) continually, with their numbers increasing each day.

Eventually, the infected fish begin to show systemic symptoms: rapid breathing, cloudy eyes, pale color, and tattered fins. In advanced cases, the white spots coalesce into patches. At this point, many people would have a difficult time even diagnosing the problem as ich.

DIAGNOSIS

Advanced aquarists learn to recognize ich very easily, but looking at a skin scrape under a microscope is the surest way to make a positive identification. Fish do develop benign white spots that can resemble ich, so the best way to differentiate between these is to make a quick sketch of where the spots are on the fish's body. If the spots seem to disappear and then reappear elsewhere, the problem is likely ich. On the other hand, if the spots remain constant in number and location, it is likely that the problem is something less serious, such as lymphocystis or minor skin lesions.

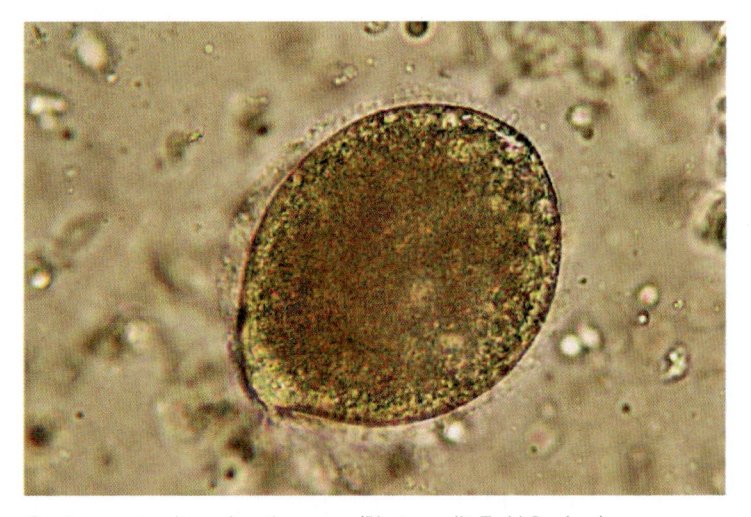

Cryptocaryon tomite under microscope (Photo credit: Todd Gardner)

TREATMENTS

Copper

The standard treatment for an active *Cryptocaryon* infection is ionic copper at 0.20 mg/l for 14 days. The proper dose is maintained by careful testing twice a day and adding enough copper solution to bring the concentration back to the proper level.

Hobbyist copper test kits are difficult to read, so public aquarists use a device called a spectrophotometer that gives much more accurate test results. Due to the difficulty in dosing, many hobbyists turn to patented organically chelated copper cures. These have a wider margin of error and often do not require testing as they are an "add-once" type of treatment. However, they are a bit slower to cure the fish and may not act quickly enough if the infection is at an advanced state.

Chloroquine

This drug is less widely available than copper but does have some potential as a medication for ich. Dosed at 8 mg/l, it serves as a preventative for all protozoan diseases. Active infections may require a dose of 15 mg/l. Treatment length varies but is generally 14 to 30 days.

Formalin

Formalin dosed at a daily rate of 25 mg/l is an old-fashioned treatment for *Cryptocaryon*, and better treatments are now available. Formalin does have a use as a dip—in this case, placing the ill fish in 166 mg/l of formalin (37% formaldehyde gas in water) for 45 minutes with good aeration. This is a stop-gap method, since moving the fish back to the original aquarium would leave it open to reinfection. It is a useful prelude to treatment in cases where the fish may have flukes at the same time.

Freshwater dips

Long touted as an easy cure for ich, use of a five-minute freshwater dip should be relegated to a diagnostic tool (as mentioned elsewhere in this guide). The popularity of this method stems from the ease of performing it, not its overall effectiveness.

Hyposalinity

Popular many years ago, hyposalinity (low salt level) treatments are less popular nowadays. These treatments often fail because aquarists are unwilling to reduce the specific gravity as low as it really needs to go (between 1.010 and 1.012 specific gravity units). Some fish cannot tolerate this low of a salt level. This treatment is very slow to cure an active infection and so is perhaps better suited as a quarantine method. The biggest risk with using a hyposalinity treatment is that another protozoan, *Uronema*, thrives in low-salinity water and is much more difficult to treat than *Cryptocaryon*.

"Tank chasing" method

A mostly theoretical method for treating *Cryptocaryon* infections takes advantage of the life cycle of the organism—moving the infected fish to a new aquarium at the point where the tomonts are produced, potentially breaking the life cycle. In real-world applications, multiple tank moves are required because, as mentioned above, the ich parasites are rarely in perfect synchronicity.

Hyper-temperature

For many years, raising the water temperature was given as one component for treating *Cryptocaryon*. The theory was that since the medications are most effective against the small tomite stage, raising the water temperature would speed up the life cycle and get the parasite to that stage sooner. This is a complete fallacy. *Cryptocaryon* actually prefers warmer temperatures, making it more difficult to treat at higher temperatures.

"Snake oil"

Treatments for *Cryptocaryon* always require that the fish be isolated from invertebrates. Ich medications that are sold as being "safe" for use with invertebrates either don't work or are actually not very safe for invertebrates. The reason that there are so many of these "snake oil" products on the market is that too many home aquarists will try anything that claims to cure ich without having to isolate the fish and invertebrates.

UV sterilizers

Ultraviolet (UV) sterilizers are also sold as a "cure" for *Cryptocaryon*. The problem is that most hobbyist-sized UV sterilizers do not have the power to make an effective kill on the relatively large *Cryptocaryon* parasite. Additionally, UV sterilizers are effective only on the tomite stage, as this is the only point where the parasite is even present in the water column.

The fallacy here is that tomites must leave the fish. Actually, some of them get caught up in the fish's mucus and stay attached until they become infective trophonts again. This means that UV sterilization will not eliminate active *Cryptocaryon* infections from a single aquarium. Where it does have benefit is in eliminating tomites as they pass through a filtration system from one discrete tank to another (like in a public aquarium or fisheries lab).

Improving water quality

Some aquarists feel that if they give their fish the "very best environment," their disease resistance will be increased so they won't be infected by ich. The problem with this idea is that it's not water quality that makes ich such a scourge in aquariums—it's the relatively small volume of aquariums that allows the tomites to locate a host so easily. Knowing all this, it's best to just develop a good plan on how you will handle *Cryptocaryon* when—not if—it rears its ugly head in your aquarium!

AMYLOODINIUM (MARINE VELVET DISEASE)

CAUSE

Commonly known as "marine velvet" in hobby parlance, *Amyloodinium* is caused by a dinoflagellate protozoan that can produce severe epidemics in home aquariums. Furthermore, it can infect fishes that are normally more resistant to other marine protozoan diseases (e.g., *Cryptocaryon*), such as sharks, rays, and eels.

SYMPTOMS

The life cycle of *Amyloodinium* is very similar to that of *Cryptocaryon*, as are the possible treatments available, but it has less distinctive early symptoms and can cause fish mortalities much sooner than other protozoan infections—sometimes within 12 hours of the onset of obvious symptoms. This disease begins as an infection of the fish's gills, and only in advanced cases does it spread to the skin, giving it a "velvety" look.

Beginning aquarists often miss the first symptoms and commonly report, "All my fish suddenly died, but the invertebrates are all fine." Since invertebrates are typically more sensitive to water-quality issues than fish are, the fact that the fish suddenly died but the invertebrates were unharmed means that water-quality problems can be ruled out. That leaves a fish disease, and *Amyloodinium* can often be diagnosed without even needing to perform a necropsy on the fish due to the rapidity of the fish loss!

DIAGNOSIS

The key to early diagnosis of *Amyloodinium* is to monitor the fish's gill health by taking regular fish respiration rates. This is a simple matter of counting the number of gill beats in one minute for a representative fish in the aquarium and then rechecking the respiration rate every few days to watch for any elevation in that rate.

Newly acquired fish that are not being treated prophylactically should have their respiration rate checked daily, as these fish are the ones at greatest risk of developing this disease. The actual respiration rate is not that important, it is a rise in the rate that must be monitored for.

Different species of fish will respire at different rates.

Smaller fish breathe faster than large ones, and fish in warmer water will respire faster as well. Typically, tropical marine fish will respire between 60 and 120 gill beats per minute. If you can't view the fish for a full minute, you can try counting for 15 seconds and multiplying the result by four.

Knowing your fish's normal baseline respiration rate is vital; any rise in that rate above 30% (and not attributable to something else, such as the fish being chased by a tankmate) should be viewed as a possible symptom of this disease.

TREATMENT

Treatments for *Amyloodinium* cannot be performed with invertebrates present, yet the entire tank usually needs to be treated in order to eradicate it. Treatment methods that have been used with good success include:

- Copper sulfate at 0.20 ppm for 14 days.
- Chloroquine at 8 to 15 ppm as a 30-day static bath.

Performing freshwater dips or lowering the tank's temperature is rarely effective. Likewise, hyposalinity treatments (sometimes recommended for *Cryptocaryon* treatments) will not work for *Amyloodinium*.

BROOKLYNELLOSIS (CLOWNFISH DISEASE)

CAUSE

Brooklynellosis is caused by a ciliated protozoan, *Brooklynella hostilis*. It very commonly affects wild-caught clownfish, thus its common name "clownfish disease." Entire shipments of wild-caught clownfish have been lost to this infection. It is also seen commonly in angelfish and anthias and sometimes in butterflyfish and tangs.

SYMPTOMS

Aquarists often miss the early symptoms of this malady in their fish, so by the time it's identified, it's often too late to save the specimen. The first signs of this disease may be limited to slightly folded fins combined with lethargy. Soon, skin mucus production increases, as does the fish's breathing rate. The fish will then lose color, stop feeding, and hang in one location, with death following in a matter of hours.

Uronema often has similar symptoms, but a reddish underlying lesion is usually associated with that disease. Bacterial infections can produce similarly cloudy skin, but they typically do not result in rapid breathing. End-stage *Cryptocaryon* can sometimes be mistaken for Brooklynellosis, as well. Positive identification requires microscopic examination of a skin scraping. Look for medium-sized, barely motile protozoans that are ventrally flattened with a slightly domed dorsal side and have cilia mostly at one end.

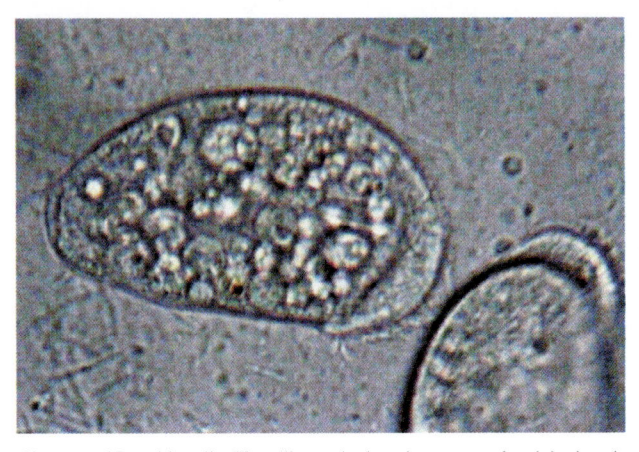

Closeup of Brooklynella: The cilia can be barely seen on the right-hand side of the organism.

TREATMENT

Few treatments are effective against Brooklynellosis, although two options include:

- A 14-day chloroquine treatment at 15 mg/l.
- Daily formalin dips at 150 ppm for 45 minutes.

Reducing the specific gravity of the treatment tank may assist the fish in balancing the electrolytes lost due to skin and gill damage. A target specific gravity of 1.018 should be maintained during treatment.

PREVENTION

Acquiring captive-raised clownfish as opposed to wild-caught ones is a good way to help prevent outbreaks of this disease. Also, Brooklynellosis is much easier to manage in a quarantine aquarium than in your main display tank.

URONEMA MARINUM (RED-BAND SYNDROME)

CAUSE

Uronema is an elongate, oval, ciliated, motile protozoan, up to 40 um in length, that can become an opportunistic pathogen in marine aquariums. Because it is so generic-looking, identification in the field is always provisional. Most professional aquarists actually mean *"Uronema-*like" when they say *"Uronema."*

Uronema infections have been seen in six families of fishes (in roughly descending order of frequency): Pomacentridae (damselfishes, specifically of the genus *Chromis*); Serranidae (subfamily Anthiinae, the anthias); Syngnathidae (seahorses and seadragons); Labridae (the wrasses); Chaetodontidae (the butterflyfishes); and, occasionally, Pomacanthidae (the angelfishes). There are, no doubt, other species of fish that can be infected.

SYMPTOMS

This moderately common protozoan disease has symptoms that include the rapid development of a red mark in the hypodermis (fat and muscle) region of the fish, often following rows of scales so that the lesion is typically elongate and angled downward as it progresses front to back along the flank of the fish. Within a day or two of the development of the primary lesion, the fish will become lethargic and stop feeding and its respiration rate will increase. Scales above the lesion can be dislodged easily due to the massive trauma to the underlying tissue.

Death follows rapidly, with few fish surviving beyond three days after the primary lesion develops.

A green chromis (*Chromis viridis*) that succumbed to red-band syndrome after 10 days in quarantine. Notice the angled red-band lesion and wide-open mouth, both common symptoms of this syndrome.

Almost universally, aquarists who do not have access to a microscope will identify this disease as a "secondary bacterial infection resulting from some injury." In fact, "capture damage" is often cited as the original cause due to the often linear nature of the lesion, which looks much like a bruise from being hit with a net frame, for example. The rapid onset of the lesion (often many days after capture) and the fact that it develops internally and then erupts externally both point to another cause.

TREATMENT

A variety of treatments have been suggested for *Uronema* infections, but full control is rarely seen following most of these treatments. Part of the issue seems to be that *Uronema* is ubiquitous (naturally occurring in marine aquariums) and re-infection is commonplace.

Bath treatments may fail because the medication used

does not target the intercellular protozoans, only those living externally on the skin of the fish. Copper treatments may reduce the numbers of these ciliates, but good control is not seen until ionic copper levels reach 0.23 ppm, and this is too close to the lethal limit for many species of fish. Formalin baths of various concentrations and durations have been proposed, but this treatment is also mostly effective against external protozoans.

The most commonly used treatment is chloroquine at 15 ppm for 30 days.

A chromis with a severe *Uronema* and bacterial infection on its tail. It was not possible to save this fish.

HYPOSALINITY AND *URONEMA*

A suspiciously high occurrence of *Uronema* outbreaks is seen in fish being kept under hyposalinity (low salinity) to control another protozoan parasite, *Cryptocaryon irritans* (saltwater ich). It seems that either *Uronema* prefers low-salinity water or such treatments lower the fish's resistance to the protozoan.

Beware using hyposalinity treatments on certain species of fish, such as this Bartlett's anthias (*Pseudanthias bartlettorum*), as they may develop red-band syndrome as a result.

PREVENTION

Uronema is much more easily prevented than cured. Once the protozoan becomes systemic within the fish's tissues, it is rarely curable. The best means for prevention seem to be to quarantine all new fish for at least 30 days, maintain a proper salinity, remove uneaten food promptly, avoid overstocking the tank, and be prepared to act swiftly and decisively if your fish become afflicted with this malady.

MONOGENEAN FLATWORMS (EYE FLUKES, GILL FLUKES, SKIN FLUKES)

CAUSE

This is a group of serious diseases that are caused by flatworms termed monogeneans (requiring only one host to complete their life cycle). Because they do not require a secondary host, they can rapidly increase their population in marine aquariums. They are often called "trematodes," but they are actually not so closely related to digenean trematodes as once thought.

Digeneans require two, or even three, hosts in order to complete their life cycle, so they rarely become a problem in marine aquariums where the required secondary host species are almost never present. Digeneans either cause no visible symptoms, or the cysted state (called metacercaria) may cause white nodules under the fish's skin on or its fins.

Monogenean worm species that commonly infect marine aquarium fish include *Neobenedenia*, *Dactylogyrus*, and *Gyrodactylus*. Let's take a more detailed look at each:

Neobenedenia melleni (eye flukes)

These are relatively large (up to 8 mm), egg-laying worms that live on the skin or eyes.

SYMPTOMS

Neobenedenia infections peak slowly; there may be no symptoms for weeks after you acquire a fish. Eventually, as the flukes multiply and grow in size, they begin to cause symptoms of disease.

The first obvious symptom may be slightly cloudy eyes, caused by the transparent fluke feeding on the eye tissue and eliciting a tissue reaction. This gives this worm the common name of "eye fluke," although it is unknown whether these worms actually prefer to feed on eye tissue, or whether that is just where they first become apparent.

As the infection becomes more serious, the fish will "flash" (scrape against objects in the tank), their skin color will become dull, their fins may become tattered, and they just generally get a "scruffy" look to them. Rapid breathing due to stress, possible secondary infection, and then death will follow if treatment is not begun.

DIAGNOSIS

The best means of diagnosis is to give the fish a five-minute freshwater dip. Not only does this knock back the infection by killing the adult parasites, but even a casual look at the bottom of the dip container afterwards will help to positively identify this disease. The worms turn whitish and fall to the bottom. Many aquarists mistake these for scales that were dislodged from the fish. However, looking at these "scales" under a dissecting microscope, or even a hand lens, will soon show them for what they are—dead worms.

A palette surgeonfish (*Paracanthurus hepatus*) receiving a freshwater dip. Note: always cover fish while they are being given a dip to keep them from jumping out and to help calm them.

Sometimes a fish's history can help diagnose at least the potential for this disease. Angelfishes and butterflyfishes are especially prone to *Neobenedenia* infections, so any of these fish that have been housed at an import facility that doesn't prophylactically treat for trematodes stand a very good chance of being infected.

Redback butterflyfish (*Chaetodon paucifasciatus*) can develop *Neobenedenia* infections.

TREATMENT

Many people suggest using a freshwater dip as a treatment for all incoming fish. The two drawbacks to this are 1) the dips are not 100% effective (and do not harm the fluke eggs) and 2) newly acquired fish often do not stand up well to the added stress of a freshwater dip when they first arrive.

Neobenedenia eggs can take 14 days or longer to hatch as motile larvae called oncomiracidium. Additionally, the eggs have sticky tendrils that attach them securely to all manner of objects in an aquarium. There is some merit to the idea of keeping a treatment tank free of substrate and siphoning the bottom regularly in order to remove some of these unhatched eggs.

Any successful treatment for these worms must be undertaken in stages. The first treatment kills off the adult worms (but not the eggs), and the subsequent treatments kill off the juvenile worms after they have all hatched but before any of them have matured and begun to lay eggs of their own. Due to variables in timing, it is virtually impossible to accomplish this in only two treatments.

Potential treatments:

- Whole-tank formalin baths at 166 ppm will eliminate the adult flukes from an aquarium but not the eggs. Because this type of treatment has no residual effect, the treatment may need to be repeated every two weeks for two or three more times. Experience in public aquarium exhibits has shown that this method rarely clears a tank completely of this pest.
- A better alternative is a praziquantel treatment at 4 ppm, followed by a 50% water change after 48 hours, then a second treatment 12 to 14 days later, followed by another 50% water change 48 hours later.

Be aware that subsequent praziquantel treatments on the same aquarium will become less and less effective. It was once thought that the worms were building immunity to the praziquantel, but some preliminary investigation shows that something else seems to be at work, likely that a population of bacteria soon grows in an aquarium that feeds on and destroys praziquantel soon after it is added to an aquarium.

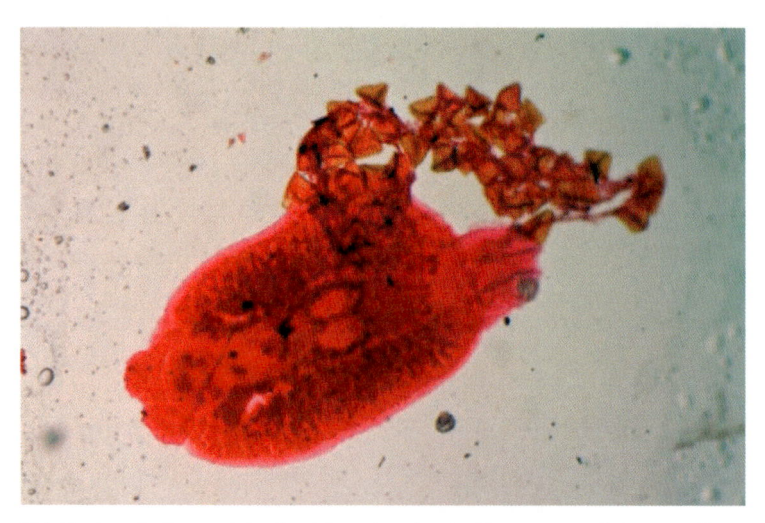

This *Neobenedenia* was stained red. It ruptured under the pressure of the coverslip. The pyramid-shaped objects are eggs that were released.

Dactylogyrus (gill flukes)

These tiny worms have four eyespots and are egg-layers. They are most often found living on a fish's gills.

SYMPTOMS

Rapid breathing is often the only obvious symptom of gill fluke infections. Secondary bacterial diseases are very common with this disease, and because the infection site is hidden by the fish's gill covers, visual identification is difficult.

DIAGNOSIS

Freshwater diagnostic dips are not an effective means to diagnose gill flukes. Due to their location deep in the gills, the fresh water is less effective. Because these worms are so small, when exposed to fresh water, they contort into tiny blobs of protoplasm. Professional aquarists will carefully snip a small gill section from a living fish and look at it under the microscope. Even then, careful examination must be made as the flukes resemble the gill lamellae of the fish. Watch for slight twitching that indicates the presence of a gill fluke.

TREATMENT

As they are egg-layers, the treatment of choice is the same as for *Neobenedenia*.

Gyrodactylus (skin flukes)

These small worms have no eyespots and are usually livebearing. Most often, they are found living on a fish's skin or fins. They are clear and typically cannot be seen with the naked eye.

SYMPTOMS

These infections start off mild, with few symptoms. As worm populations increase, the fish will be seen flashing. The fins may become tattered, and the skin may develop a dull look. Only severe cases are fatal due to the worms themselves; usually secondary bacterial infections are the cause of death.

DIAGNOSIS

Because these worms are small, freshwater dips do not work well as a diagnostic tool. After such a dip, the worms contort into tiny blobs that are difficult for most aquarists to identify. Looking at a skin scrape under a microscope is a much better method, as the flukes can be seen moving around.

TREATMENT

Praziquantel is the treatment of choice. Because these worms are livebearers, there is no resistant egg stage to worry about. Generally, an effective treatment is to dose the praziquantel at 2.2 mg/l, then, after 72 hours, change 50% of the water and re-dose with the same amount.

Many home aquarists buy cleaner wrasses, neon gobies, or cleaner shrimp in the hope that these animals will clear their fish of parasites. This is simply never effective for bacterial or protozoan infections. However, with some large parasites, notably copepods and *Neobenedenia*, partial control may be seen.

Scarlet skunk cleaner shrimp (*Lysmata amboinensis*) are cleaners, but they cannot control disease outbreaks in your fish.

"Who cleans the cleaner" is the biggest issue. Cleaner

wrasses are notoriously delicate in captivity, with 40-day mortality rates usually above 90%. If you wish to experiment with this control method, only acquire cleaner wrasses that have been collected off the east coast of Africa—for some reason, these survive much better in captivity. Be aware that some dealers have recognized this and sell all of their cleaner wrasses as "African."

Do not rely on cleaner wrasses (*Labroides dimidiatus*) to control disease outbreaks in your other fish.

TURBELLARIAN INFECTION (BLACK SPOT DISEASE, BLACK ICH, TANG DISEASE)

Turbellarians are a group of worms related to trematodes. They often go undiagnosed as a cause of active infections in fishes except for one group: *Paravortex* sp.

CAUSE AND SYMPTOMS

Since this disease is often seen in newly acquired fish, the suspicion is that the fish bring the disease with them and become infected due to the transport stress they endure.

This parasite causes very distinctive black spots on some species of fish, most notably tangs and surgeonfish. Other fish that may become infected with *Paravortex* include butterflyfishes, angelfishes, gobies, and jawfishes.

The worm encysts under the fish's skin, and the fish deposits black melanin pigment as a reaction to the infection. Since these spots are so apparent to even the casual observer, this disease is easily diagnosed, even by beginning aquarists.

OFTEN SELF-LIMITING

The problem is that this sometimes causes the aquarist to overreact and begin a treatment that actually might be more harmful than the disease itself. It turns out that many cases of *Paravortex* infection are self-limiting; unless tank conditions are very poor, the worms often die out and the infection goes away on its own.

Only if the spots increase greatly in number (more than 20 spots on a fish) or the fish begin showing other signs of ill health should a treatment be undertaken.

CLEANLINESS COUNTS

Some aquarists have reported that careful siphon-cleaning of the aquarium substrate and improving overall cleanliness in the aquarium helps to reduce this infection. It is possible that *Paravortex* has a non-parasitic, free-living form at one stage of its life cycle and that careful cleaning will remove the parasite at that point.

SOME TURBELLARIANS ARE TOUGHER TO DIAGNOSIS

There are other turbellarians that do not cause melanistic skin changes in fish and are much more difficult to diagnose. *Ichthyophaga* is one type known to infect marine fishes that can cause significant fish loss in crowded conditions. Diagnosis of this parasite generally requires a skin scrape.

It's also noteworthy that treatment with freshwater dips may contort the worm's body shape so much that positive identification is difficult. In some cases, no real symptoms are seen until fish loss occurs. Under the microscope, look for an oval-shaped worm with a pair of dark eyespots.

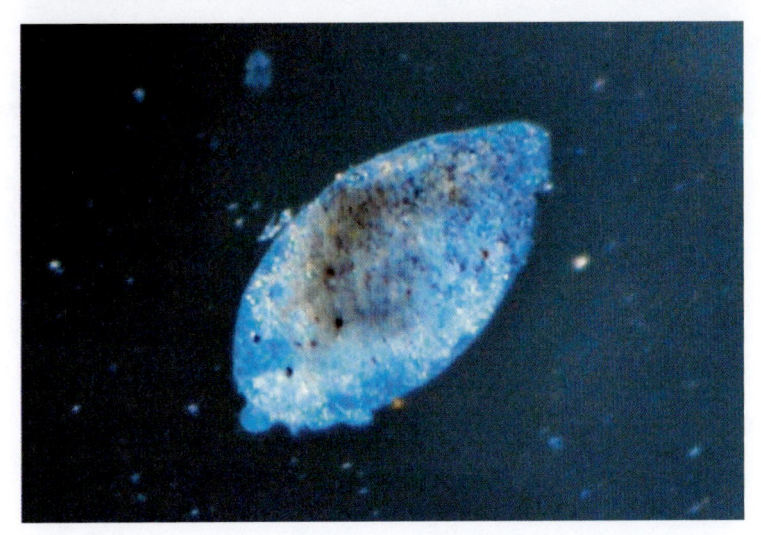

A turbellarian removed from a fish by a freshwater dip. Notice the twin eyespots at the left end of the organism.

TREATMENT OPTIONS

Because turbellarians cause a fairly deep-seated infection, they are difficult to remove using freshwater dips or other topical treatments. Other treatment options that have been utilized with varying degrees of effectiveness include:

- Praziquantel at 2 mg/l is a safe, commonly used treatment for this malady, but for some reason, it is not always effective.
- A 45-minute formalin dip at 166 ppm can be effective, but then the fish must be moved to a non-infected aquarium.
- Chloroquine at 15 ppm has been shown to be an effective treatment, but some fish may experience toxic reactions at this dose.
- Organophosphate pesticides, such as trichlorfon (Dylox), have been the treatment of choice for many years but cannot be recommended due to their potential toxicity to humans.
- Copper treatments are ineffective, at least at the concentrations well tolerated by fish.

PARASITIC CRUSTACEANS (COPEPODS, ISOPODS, AND SEA LICE)

CAUSE

This disease problem is caused by a variety of very small crustaceans that can parasitize fish. Some are obligate parasites with specific host species, while others are generalists and can live separate from a fish and only return periodically in order to feed on the fish's skin. The different species have a wide variety of body shapes, but because they are all arthropods, they always have jointed legs and segmented body parts.

Non-parasitic amphipods, copepods, and isopods are also common cryptic inhabitants of aquariums. Seen as little white specks moving about the aquarium glass, these creatures (often called "pods" by aquarists) are harmless but sometimes indicate that the primary inhabitants (the fish) are being overfed.

"POD" CHARACTERISTICS

Amphipods tend to be flattened side to side and have two different types of legs. None of these are parasitic.

Copepods are flattened top to bottom, and non-parasitic ones often have large antennae. In parasitic species, the antennae are replaced with grasping hooks. So, if you see a large number of copepods, all with large antennae and not attached to a fish, they aren't parasitic (though the parasitic species are free-swimming during the copepodite stage).

A copepod removed from a marine fish by a formalin dip.

Isopods tend to have legs that are all the same ("iso" means "same," and "pod" means "foot"). They are also either cylindrical or flattened top to bottom. The cirolanid isopods look a bit like pill bugs that you can find in your garden, but they are known parasites of fish.

Top view of an isopod found infecting fish.

SYMPTOMS

Symptoms of copepod infestation can be a bit too general and vague for beginning aquarists to discern very readily. The fish may flash, act nervously, or breathe heavily. In severe infestations, the fish's skin will develop blood spots and the fins may become tattered.

In older aquariums that have a high bioload (large number of fish), an aggressive type of copepod may take up residence. These creatures hide in the gravel and under rocks during the day and swim up into the water column at night to feed on the fish's skin. Fish in aquariums with an infestation of this type of copepod will be seen hovering near the surface, as far away from the substrate as possible. They may also show other signs of stress, such as pale coloration, jerking movements, and rapid breathing.

DIAGNOSIS

Some crustacean parasites, including many of the isopods, are easily seen with the naked eye. In other instances, the female's twin egg sacs can be seen emerging from under the fish's skin. Branchiurans (*Argulus*) can sometimes be seen by observant aquarists, but as they are clear, their 10 mm bodies don't stand out too well.

In other cases, such as with *Ergasilus*, the parasites are too small to be seen directly, so you need to look for secondary symptoms as mentioned above. A diagnostic dip will aid in the identification of these pests. The dip also serves as a temporary treatment, as it rids the fish of most of the parasites attached to it at that moment.

TREATMENT

The most frequently suggested treatment for crustacean parasites is the application of an organophosphate pesticide, such as trichlorfon. These products are too dangerous for home use, so other treatments need to be used.

The best way to deal with these parasites in the home aquarium is through a series of dips—formalin at 166 ppm for 45 minutes or fresh water for 5 to 7 minutes. Two difficulties are seen with this method, however. First, returning the fish directly to the infected tank allows for rapid reinfection. Second, these parasites have pinching mouthparts that make them difficult to dislodge during a dip.

One method used by public aquariums is to give the entire aquarium a high-dose (166 ppm) bath with formalin. After about 30 minutes, the tank is very quickly drained to 20% full. Previously mixed salt water is then added to the tank to refill it. This process exposes the fish to about 45 minutes of formalin above 150 ppm and then leaves a residual formalin dose in the tank of 33 ppm, which is generally tolerated as a constant bath by most fish.

Obviously, this cannot be done in aquariums where invertebrates are present, and it does require a substantial amount of salt water. Furthermore, a second treatment is often required. For reef aquariums, removing the fish to a treatment tank and allowing the main aquarium to lie fallow for six weeks is the best treatment.

A scad with a huge isopod removed from its gill chamber. The isopod made room for itself as it grew by eating away portions of the fish's gill chamber. This single parasite proved fatal to the fish.

BACTERIAL INFECTIONS

Bacterial infections are by far the most difficult diseases for home aquarists to deal with. Since you cannot see bacteria with the naked eye, any symptom without a known cause can be mistakenly attributed to bacterial infection. Additionally, secondary bacterial infections (described below) get their start after another problem—which must be resolved first—is already present. Finally, fish are difficult to dose properly with antibiotics, and an aquarium's biofilter is often compromised when antibiotics are used. If the biofilter is "nuked," the resulting high ammonia levels may do more harm to the fish than the bacterial disease itself.

Also, many aquarists have difficulty assessing the outcome of a bacterial disease in their fish. If the infected fish is treated and survives, they automatically assume the treatment must have cured it. In actuality, however, some bacterial infections are self-resolving, and the affected fish manage to heal themselves. This often results in people advocating for "herbal" cures and other dubious treatments—they may have seemed to work, but the fish simply survived in spite of the "cure."

Indiscriminate use of antibiotics has also been implicated in creating resistant strains of pathogenic bacteria, so any treatments need to be carefully considered before applying them.

Primary bacterial infections (fish tuberculosis [*Mycobacterium marinum*] and bacterial kidney and gill diseases)

CAUSE

Rarely, bacterial diseases will infect marine aquarium fish without some other predisposing factor (see secondary infections below). These problems are more often seen in fish hatcheries, where many fish are housed under crowded conditions.

SYMPTOMS

Bacterial gill disease will cause the fish to respire quickly, often with no other symptoms. *Mycobacterium marinum* is a very common disease in older aquarium fish. In fact, most fish that die from "old age" are found to be harboring the organism that causes fish tuberculosis.

This freshwater cichlid shows symptoms of *Mycobacterium* infection: poor muscle tone, swollen abdomen, poor color, and protruding eyes.

DIAGNOSIS

As these infections are not evident by observing the fish, the only reliable method for diagnosing them is culturing tissue taken during the necropsy of the fish. When the suspected bacteria is grown on a petri dish, small wafers of different antibiotics are added to the plate. When a "zone of inhibition" is seen around a particular disk, that drug is probably the best means of treatment.

TREATMENT

The only effective treatment for these diseases is administering injectable, or perhaps oral, antibiotics (see formulary).

Secondary bacterial infections (*Pseudomonas*, *Staphylococcus*, *Vibrio*, and related bacteria)

CAUSE

These are opportunistic infections caused by bacteria that

are always present in aquariums. Such infections are always associated with bacterial blooms due to poor water quality, damage from some prior disease, or injury from shipping or tankmate aggression. Rarely, spoiled fish food can cause internal bacterial infections.

SYMPTOMS

A variety of symptoms may be present: red patches (petechiae) on the skin are commonly observed. The fish may show fin erosion from the initial damage as well as the subsequent bacteria feeding on the tissue. White, cloudy skin, fins, or eyes are fairly commonly seen as well.

A clownfish with severe bacterial fin rot of its caudal fin. It did not recover. Notice how the hypural plate (tail bone) is affected. Fish cannot regrow their lost fins once that much damage has occurred.

DIAGNOSIS

Positive diagnosis is the same as with primary bacterial diseases and is outside the scope of home aquarists.

TREATMENT

First, the original cause of the injury must be resolved. Once that has been achieved, the fish may recover on its own or it may need to be moved to a hospital tank and treated with antibiotics.

In every case, the first antibiotic to try is a broad-spectrum one that works on gram-negative types of bacteria (see formulary). Beware of "hunting" for a cure; antibiotics usually take five to seven days to effect a cure. Many aquarists, not seeing any improvement after a day or so, will try a different drug, and then, perhaps, another. This is a mistake. Make your best choice and stay with it for a full course of therapy.

This cardinalfish succumbed to a combination of protozoan and bacterial infections that became active when its tail was damaged by tankmate aggression.

FUNGAL INFECTIONS

Fungi (plural of fungus) are a group of organisms

differentiated from plants and animals by their chitinous cell walls. Included in this group are the familiar mushrooms and yeast. Freshwater aquarists are all too familiar with external fungal infections caused by *Saprolegnia*. Also called water mold, this infection causes white, cottony-looking growths on the skin of fish. The primary treatment for this disease is adding salt to the water, so it's no wonder that these infections are rarely seen in marine fish.

However, infrequent as they are, fungal infections do show up in marine fishes from time to time. The symptoms are different from those of freshwater fishes, though; marine fish will develop an open sore with raised scales around the edge. The sore may be very deep, penetrating deep into the muscle tissue or body cavity. The center of these lesions is usually tan or brown, and a skin scrape taken will often show fungal hyphae (looking like tiny bundles of straw) mixed with bacteria and sometimes protozoans.

These deep-seated, multi-disease infections are extremely difficult to treat but are, luckily, quite rare. One possible treatment is giving daily 45-minute formalin baths at a concentration of 150 to 166 ppm. If the fish is moved to a treatment tank, a static formalin bath of 25 ppm can be used, possibly in conjunction with antibiotics to help control the concurrent bacterial infection.

An internal fungus, *Ichthyophonus hoferi*, has also been reported in marine fishes. Symptoms of this malady are indistinct but can include lethargy, mild exophthalmia, and darkened skin. Onset is slow but progressive, and the disease is usually fatal. Positive diagnosis can be made only by post-mortem examination of the infected fish's internal organs under a microscope. There is no effective home treatment for this disease other than to isolate the infected fish.

INTERNAL PARASITES

CAUSE

A variety of organisms can infect fish internally. Most are worms, a few are protozoans, and there is even an eel that infects the heart of living sharks! Some species have complicated life cycles with intermediate hosts, and others can directly infect fish.

Nematodes can infect the gut of marine fish, causing very serious infections. Tapeworms (cestodes) may also be present but do not reproduce without a second host, so they are rarely a problem. Gut protozoans, such as *Hexamita*, are normally present in most fish but sometimes cause disease when their populations grow as a result of the fish's immune response being limited by some stress factor.

Hexamita was once implicated in causing Head and Lateral Line Erosion, but its presence in the guts of fish with HLLE was purely coincidental. If non-infected fish had been examined, *Hexamita* would have been found in them as well.

Sporozoans, such as myxosporidians and microsporidians, can internally infect fish. They can also create external lesions called xenomas. One of the more commonly seen, called *Glugea*, creates white, smooth masses inside and outside of infected fish. Some people may mistake these growths for *Cryptocaryon*, but any spot that stays in the same position on a fish for more than a few days is not *Cryptocaryon*. There is no treatment for sporozoans, but luckily they are a relatively rare affliction in aquarium fishes.

Interestingly, flashlight fish often house a pair of trematodes in their gall bladder. These metazoans seem to be commensal; they do not increase in number and are seen in apparently healthy fish.

SYMPTOMS

Symptoms of internal parasites, like the causative organisms themselves, are varied. The most important visual symptom is emaciation—abnormal thinness of the fish's belly and the nape (behind the head). If this is present and the fish is feeding well, then internal parasites of the gut may be competing with the fish for that food. Other symptoms include white, stringy feces and bloating of the abdomen.

Look closely at this fish above its ventral fin and below its pectoral fin. Even from this side view, it is evident that the specimen is moderately emaciated.

DIAGNOSIS

Internal parasites are extremely difficult to diagnose visually based on symptoms alone. As with bacterial infections (which are too small to see), these internal infections are often attributed to any problem in a fish that involves mucus being excreted with feces. Also, abnormal thinness can often be attributed to the fish not feeding well in the first place—it may be a species that does not feed well on normal aquarium fare and has no internal worms at all.

Looking at a fecal sample under a microscope may help with diagnosis, but understand that any fecal matter deposited in an aquarium will become contaminated with all sorts of free-living protozoans and metazoans in a matter of an hour or so. If possible, collect a fish's feces while it is being held in a clean container.

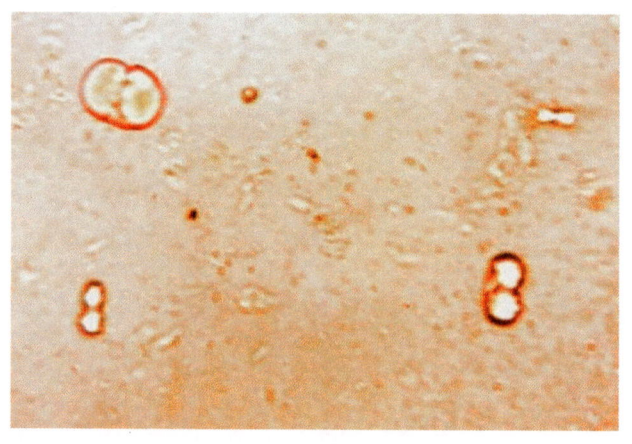

Possible myxosporidians from internal tissue of a fish.

TREATMENT OPTIONS

Wait out "self-limiting" parasites

As alluded above, many internal parasites require additional hosts to complete their life cycle. In aquariums, these hosts are almost never present, so the disease is considered "self-limiting." That is, once the adult parasite dies, the fish is free of the disease because no new parasites are being produced. In other words, the "parasite load" never gets any higher than when the fish arrived in your aquarium. In such cases (like tapeworm infections), it is safest to just wait.

Some internal parasites have direct development; they do not need a secondary host and may not even need to leave the fish in order to complete their life cycle. These parasites, such as some nematodes, can become very serious infections and must be treated if possible.

Medicated foods

Medicated foods would seem to be the favored treatment option, but all are dosed as a percent of medication in the food, fed to the fish at a rate that is a proportion of the fish's body weight. The trouble, of course, is that few aquarists know the weight of their fish.

Avoid the advice to soak the fish's food with medication. This can never work except by dumb luck. Think about it; nobody knows how much of the medication actually soaks into the food (if any), and then, since you don't know the weight of the fish, the amount of food to feed is just a guess.

Garlic

One treatment that has found much favor with home aquarists is the use of garlic as a food additive. It is relatively non-toxic, so dosage errors are not dangerous to the fish. However, it is more of an "irritant" to internal parasites, dislodging some, but not all of them. Its use should be considered a therapy as opposed to a medical treatment. The amount of garlic to be used is not well defined, but there are commercial products available to use for soaking food.

Medicating the water

Since, by definition, these parasites are internal, external bath medications won't easily reach them. However, marine fish do "drink" water in order to help maintain a proper osmotic balance, so medications added to the water itself do end up inside the fish—but at an unknown dosage. Still, there is some anecdotal evidence that praziquantel, dosed at 2.2 to 4 mg/l, can help eliminate internal parasites in marine fish.

VIRAL DISEASES

Viruses (singular viron) are small infectious bodies that replicate themselves inside the cells of living things. Different types of viruses infect a wide range of organisms: animals, plants, fungi, and even bacteria. They possess some characteristics of living organisms and are affected by natural selection, but they cannot replicate themselves without first infecting the cell of a host animal's body. A typical virus is many times smaller than even the smallest bacteria cell and is much too small to be seen through a regular microscope.

Viral infections can spread between fish in different ways, but ingestion and direct contact with viruses in the water are the two common modes of transmission. Some viruses will infect only particular species, while others can infect a wider range of different fish. A teaspoon of sea water can contain over one million virons (Shors 2008). Most of this count are bacteriophages, viruses that infect bacteria. These are harmless to animals and plants but are important in the aquatic carbon cycle.

It is thought that some viral infections can infect a fish but lie dormant. Then, if the fish is later stressed due to poor water quality, overcrowding, or damage due to handling, the disease becomes an active infection. This is similar to how a cold sore activates when a person is stressed.

In other instances, the fish develops disease symptoms immediately upon infection, the way people do when they catch a cold.

SYMPTOMS OF VIRAL DISEASE IN MARINE AQUARIUM FISHES

The symptoms of viral infections in fish overlap with many other diseases, so positive identification is difficult with home aquarium fishes. Just as with humans, some fish viral infections are more deadly than others. It is probable that many fish viral diseases go unreported because their symptoms do not include extensive mortality.

The table below lists potential symptoms that might arise in infected fish. Note that survivors of viral diseases may show no symptoms at all but can still possibly infect new fish added to the aquarium. Don't make viral diseases a scapegoat for all problems with your aquarium fish. Because the symptoms are so varied (including death with no apparent symptoms), it is very easy for home aquarists to attribute just about any fish loss to viral disease. The reality is that viral diseases of fish cannot be accurately diagnosed without very specialized laboratory testing that is outside the capability of home aquarists.

- Light gray granular growths on fin edges or, less commonly, the fish's body.
- External tumors.
- Pale gills (indicates anemia).+

- Symptoms of nerve damage: darkened skin, sluggishness, and disorientation.
- White, stringy feces. +
- Only one sort of fish in an aquarium being affected.
- Pop-eye in both eyes. +
- Bloody fins or skin. +
- Very young fish affected more severely than adult fish.
- Swollen abdomen (ascites). +
- Sudden death with no previous observable symptoms.
- Newly acquired fish showing symptoms, followed by older fish. +

Symptoms marked with a "+" are also commonly seen with other, more common diseases, so misdiagnosis is highly likely.

HOW MANY VIRUSES AFFECT FISH?

Over 125 viral diseases have been identified in fishes, but this is more a function of where scientists look for them. Most identified fish viruses have been found in aquacultured food fishes, as that is where the time and money is being spent. While some vaccines have been developed to protect food fishes from specific viral infections, just like with the common cold, there is no cure for an active viral infection in fishes.

Marine aquarium hobbyists can and do encounter viruses in their fishes, the most notable are:

AQUABIRNAVIRUSES

This viral group causes a number of severe diseases in aquacultured food fishes but has also been isolated from fish in public aquariums. It has a wide range of hosts, including some invertebrates. Symptoms vary depending on the type of virus involved, but the take-away message is to adequately quarantine all newly acquired fish in order to help protect existing fish populations from incoming, unidentified viral infections.

BANGGAI CARDINALFISH IRIDOVIRUS (BCIR)

This disease was originally discovered in 1933 but then lost to science for about 60 years, when the Banggai cardinalfish (*Pterapogon kauderni*) was "rediscovered" and began entering the tropical fish trade. Aquarists noted how hardy the species was and that they were very easy to reproduce in captivity. A decade later, the price for wild-caught Banggai cardinalfish had decreased fivefold, but the animals were now considered very delicate, with high losses seen in newly acquired wild fish.

What was the cause of this sudden change in the apparent health of this species in captivity? Poor handling, collection with cyanide (unlikely), and bacterial disease were all suggested as possible reasons for this change. A researcher then published a study showing that the presence of an iridovirus was associated with episodes of mass mortality in newly imported cardinalfish (Weber et al. 2009). A similar virus has since been isolated from the common batfish, *Platax orbicularis* (Sriwanayos et al. 2013), but a corresponding high mortality in aquarium fish of that species has not been noted, perhaps because many fewer batfish are imported for the pet trade than the ever-popular Banggai cardinalfish.

Since there is no cure for this viral disease, captive-raised fish that were never exposed to wild stock, or fish that have subsequently developed immunity by surviving an infection would be the best choices for home aquarists. Avoid inexpensive wild-caught Banggai cardinalfish. Not only do they have a poor survival record, but they're also being collected at such a high rate that wild populations are locally threatened with extinction.

HLLE AND VIRAL DISEASE

One research project correlated the development of Head and Lateral Line Erosion (HLLE, discussed in detail in Chapter 3) with the presence of a reovirus in marine angelfish (Varner and Lewis 1991). However, this study did not clearly show that the virus caused the HLLE; the problem may just have been coincidental to the angelfish being infected with the virus.

Transmission of HLLE by an infectious agent was not duplicated in a subsequent study, which showed that the use of activated lignite carbon was the causative agent in the development of HLLE in a group of surgeonfish (Hemdal and Odum 2011). HLLE lesions in marine fishes have never been demonstrated to be infectious (i.e., moving an infected fish into an aquarium with symptom-free fish does not result in a spread of the infection).

Since showing an infectious nature of a viral disease is the one primary diagnostic tool, it is extremely unlikely that HLLE is directly caused by a virus. Much more likely, the HLLE lesions weaken the fish's immune system, making the fish more susceptible to viral infections.

LYMPHOCYSTIS (CAULIFLOWER DISEASE)

This is a common viral disease of marine, brackish, and certain freshwater fishes (usually those with marine relatives: glassfish and rainbowfish). It is a chronic (long-lasting) but self-limiting (usually going away on its own) syndrome caused by an iridovirus. The virus causes hypertrophy (enlargement) of the epithelial cells of a fish's skin and fins.

Initial symptoms consist of off-white to gray nodules on the fish that spread and grow larger over a timeframe of 10 to 90 days. Commonly, when a lymphocystis nodule forms on a pectoral fin, a new nodule will soon begin to form on the part of the fish that is brushed by the fin, indicating that direct contact can be a mode of spreading the infection.

When lymphocystis first starts, the small growths can be misdiagnosed as a protozoan infection, such as *Cryptocaryon*, or even a bacterial infection. The fact that the lesions are long-lasting and do not cause the fish to become acutely ill rules out these more virulent diseases.

Excess mucus on the fin of a fire clown looks like lymphocystis, but it isn't.

Since lymphocystis is most often seen in newly imported fish, capture and transport stresses are often mentioned as the stressors that allow this disease to take hold. While this may be true, it may also be that the cause is actually exposure to other infected fish in the aquarium systems of the exporter, importer, or retail suppliers. In any event, it is extremely rare for a fish held in captivity for more than four to six months to suddenly develop this disease.

Treatment with copper sulfate has also been implicated in the development of lymphocystis in marine fish. The connection is actually not very clear, in that copper sulfate is most often used on newly imported fish, and those are the ones that develop the disease most often.

Lymphocystis infections can sometimes become more serious, covering large areas of a fish's body and even interfering with proper feeding if the cell growth involves areas around the mouth. In rare instances, the virus can also cause enlargement of the cells of internal organs, especially in marine fish (Wolf 1988). This has the potential of causing serious yet difficult-to-identify diseases in marine fish.

A variety of cures have been suggested for this disease over the years. Some public aquarists have reported that a reduction in the animal's environmental stress level will help reduce the severity of an infection. Others have reported that treatment with a mixture of malachite green and formalin (Quick Cure, Formalite, etc.) helps limit the spread of the lesions. Since both of these compounds can damage an aquarium's biofilter, and since both are toxic to fish, care must be taken if this method is attempted. By far, the most commonly recommended treatment involves surgically removing the hypertrophied skin cells, followed with a topical antibiotic to hopefully prevent secondary bacterial infection.

The issue with all these suggested treatments is that because lymphocystis is usually self-limiting, remission of the disease will almost always occur in spite of any treatment undertaken. Additionally, cutting the tissue to remove the lesions releases viral particles into the aquarium, potentially spreading the disease to other fish. Finally, any time a fish is handled, there is a risk to its health due to injury or infection.

Close-up of a severe case of lymphocystis on the fin of a seabass.

The general advice is to never intercede with a lymphocystis infection—just let it run its course. The only exception might be if the fish develops a severe form of the disease and its mouth develops lesions that might inhibit it from feeding. Even in those extreme cases, surgery around the mouth will also cause the fish to stop feeding, so it may be better to just wait it out (Hemdal 2014).

Interestingly, aquarists do not seem to report lymphocystis infections in their fish as often as they did in the 1970's and 80's. Anecdotally, the disease does not seem as common in public aquariums overall as it used to be. The reason(s) for this change are unclear. It may be that more aquarists are familiar with the syndrome, know that it is usually self-limiting, and therefore do not report it. It may also be that marine fish traveling through the commercial supply chain are being handled better, with less stress, making the outbreaks less common.

The table below (adapted from Hemdal 2014) lists the marine aquarium fish groups known to be vulnerable to the lymphocystis virus (+ = can occur, ++ = commonly infects, +++ = extremely common).

Common Name	Taxonomic Group	Prevalence
Angelfish (marine)	Pomacanthidae	++
Blennies	Blenniidae	+
Boxfish	Ostraciidae	++
Butterflyfish	Chaetodontidae	++
Damselfish, clownfish	Pomacentridae	+
Dottybacks	Pseudochromidae	+
Gobies	Gobiidae	+
Groupers	Serranidae	+
Hamlets	*Hypoplectrus* spp.	+++
Moorish idol	Zanclidae	++
Porcupine fish	Diodontidae	+
Rabbitfish	Siganidae	+
Royal gramma	Serranidae	+++
Scorpionfish, lionfish	Scorpaeniformes	+
Tangs, surgeonfish	Acanthuridae	+
Triggerfish	Balistidae	++
Wrasses	Labridae	++

No doubt lymphocystis will infect marine fish other than those species on this list, but it's a good starting point of known carriers of this disease. Some marine aquarium fish are so commonly affected with lymphocystis that diagnosis can be made just knowing that they are the species involved. If an aquarist says they see a growth on a royal gramma, copperband butterflyfish, or hamlet that they just acquired, it is very likely to be lymphocystis.

CONTROL OF VIRAL DISEASES

If you suspect that a fish under your care is infected with a viral disease, the best course of action is to limit the potential for its spread to other fish. Isolating all possible means of transmission is the first thing to do. Items such as tank tools and nets that are exposed to the water in an aquarium suspected of being infected with a virus should be disinfected before being brought into contact with water in another aquarium.

Another way that viral particles can move from one aquarium to another is by aerosolization. Life-support equipment (air pumps and filters) often sends tiny air bubbles up out of an aquarium into the air. These bubbles can drift to nearby aquariums. Viral particles are so small that they can be carried along with the air bubble to a nearby tank.

Since there is no cure for viral diseases in marine fish, the best you can do is provide the ailing fish the finest care possible during the infection in the hopes that it will recover on its own once the fish's cells build up antibodies to the viral particles. Moving the fish to a hospital tank is usually not advisable. The ill fish has already shed virons into the aquarium's water, exposing tankmates to the same disease, and hospital tanks are almost always a more stressful environment for the fish than the aquarium it had been residing in.

The only exception to this would be if there had been

incidences of aggression in the main aquarium that were the stress factor that precipitated the infection—then it may be more appropriate to remove the infected fish. It's better to manage the environment through water changes, a steady temperature, high quality food, and good aeration.

It should be added that it has been discovered that the spread of some viral diseases of game fishes is temperature-dependent and they do not grow well at temperatures outside of a particular range. However, changing the temperature of the water is a difficult means to control viral diseases in tropical marine fish because the fish have as narrow a survivable temperature range as the viruses do.

THE FUTURE

About a dozen vaccines have been developed and approved for use in fishes, but only for particular viral diseases of salmon, carp, bass, and catfish. It is unlikely that vaccines will be developed for marine aquarium fishes in the near future because the process is so expensive. The marine aquarium business is very disseminated, with many small companies producing products. For that reason, extensive research and development is simply not available. Adding to this is the unfortunate "disposable fish" syndrome, where hobbyists and dealers alike apparently find it more cost effective to replace a fish than to keep it alive by giving it expensive care.

Dr. Roy P. E. Yanong of the University of Florida has

written a very informative paper on vaccines of warmwater fishes: http://bit.ly/yanong-vaccines

EXOPHTHALMIA AND OTHER EYE DISEASES

You've likely heard the well-known proverb, "The eyes are the window to the soul." This actually is a particularly appropriate phrase when diagnosing fish health problems.

Very often, the first sign of an external disease in a fish is a change in the structure, color, clarity, or shape of its eyes. It is not so much that the fish's eyes are affected by disease first, just that early changes in the outer body of a fish often show up better on the clear tissue of the eye. Knowing how these eye changes can be used to identify fish diseases is a very helpful skill in an aquarist's arsenal of diagnostic tools.

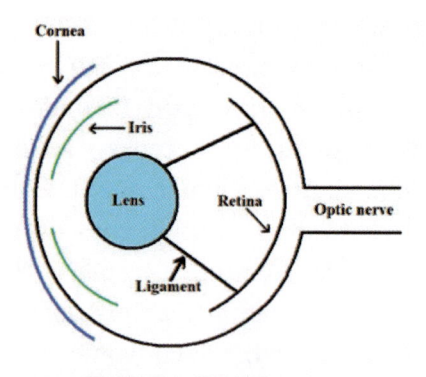

Simplified Diagram of a Fish Eye

A variety of health issues can involve the eyes of a fish, ranging from a slight cloudiness to enucleation—the loss of the entire eye. Knowing whether the problem affects one or both eyes is very important. If the problem affects just one of a fish's eyes, the cause is likely to be a specific injury to that eye alone. If both eyes are equally affected, the problem is not likely to be a simple injury and there is more of a chance that the problem is systemic—involving the entire fish or, in the case of multiple animals showing the same symptom, the entire aquarium.

Most eye examinations in captive fish must be performed while they are swimming in an aquarium. A small, blue LED penlight may help illuminate the eye of the fish, assuming it doesn't swim away too quickly. A more comprehensive exam can be performed if the fish can be sedated and held out of the water for a moment. In these cases, the blue LED penlight can be held at an angle to the eye, causing any ulcers to create shadows, giving them better definition. Veterinarians can also use fluorescein dye to create even greater contrast in the eye lesions.

CLOUDY EYES

If a fish's eye seems cloudy, the first task is to determine whether it may be normal for that species. Some puffers, rabbitfish, and scorpionfish have a normal cloudy sheen to their eyes. This will be seen in both eyes equally and will always be present under the right viewing conditions. It the cloudiness appears over time, it is not a normal condition for that fish.

Some fish, such as this scorpionfish, have naturally cloudy lenses in their eyes.

The next thing to determine is whether the cloudiness is on the eye's surface (on the surface of the cornea) or deeper inside the organ (involving the pupil). A fish with one eye that has a cloudy cornea has likely just injured the eye, and time will often heal the problem (assuming no secondary bacterial infection arises). A fish (or multiple fish) with both eyes having cloudy corneas usually indicates a systemic problem. This may be poor water quality, a bacterial or protozoan infection, or, very often, a trematode (fluke) infection.

DISEASE-INDUCED EYE PROBLEMS

Bacterial diseases

If a fish gradually develops only minor bilateral pop-eye (usually without cloudiness to the cornea), a bacterial disease may be the cause. Fish tuberculosis, *Mycobacterium marinum*, is a very common chronic disease that can cause this. This bacteria is ubiquitous—that is, it is commonly found in aquarium water, soil, and even in many frozen fish foods. Some species of fish are more prone to becoming infected than others, and there is no proven treatment for this malady. Additional symptoms of this problem can include emaciation (loss of body mass despite the fish feeding well), darker-than-normal coloration, rapid breathing, and lethargy. In marine fish, it is generally a "disease of old age," so only long-term captive fish seem to succumb to it.

If an external bacterial disease is suspected, gentamicin sulfate, an aminoglycoside antibiotic, has been shown to help. Because this antibiotic is applied topically and is water-soluble, it is probably better to use the ophthalmic ointment as opposed to the aqueous solution, as the latter will immediately wash off the fish's eyes when the animal is returned to the water. Some aquarists have reported using this drug in conjunction with dorzolamide hydrochloride (Trusopt) in cases of external bacterial eye infections combined with mild exophthalmia. Trusopt is a carbonic anhydrase inhibitor used in humans to reduce ocular hypertension. It is presumed that this drug may have a similar effect on eye swelling in fishes.

Fungal disease

External fungal diseases are extremely rare in marine fishes, but *Saprolegnea* sp. is a fungus that will often infect freshwater fishes at the site of a previous injury. In most cases, the individual threads, or hyphae, are visible to the naked eye or by using a simple hand lens.

There is some debate about the need to control *Saprolegnea*. This fungus feeds on dead tissue, which might otherwise become infected with bacteria. Some aquarists advocate leaving it alone to "clean" the wound. If the wound is so severe that the fungus takes over, the fish would have died from the injury anyway.

At issue here is that a fungal infection on the fish's eye may leave scarring that would affect the fish's ability to see. Anti-fungal treatments may be warranted in these cases, either methylene blue at 2 ppm or sea salt at 4 ppt (if the freshwater fish will tolerate that level).

But again, *Saprolegnea* is not a disease marine aquarium hobbyists are going to encounter.

Gas bubble disease

This syndrome most typically produces gas bubbles on the body of seahorses (including the male's brood pouch) but can also involve the skin around the eyes. The cause of this problem is not well known, and only experimental treatments have been proposed.

Injections with acetazolamide at around 5 mg per kg have shown promise in treating this disease, but that treatment is an off-label use of the drug and outside the ability of most home aquarists to perform.

Many aquarists have attributed this syndrome to supersaturation of the water with gas—making it an environmental condition (covered below). However, it has been repeatedly shown that gas bubble disease can infect seahorses in aquarium systems that are not undergoing supersaturation, so the cause of the problem must be found elsewhere.

Parasites

Cryptocaryon irritans (marine ich or whitespot disease) can cause cloudy eyes, but there are always secondary symptoms, such as distinct white spots on the fish's body.

Trematodes (flukes) will very often cause cloudy eyes as the primary symptom. *Neobenedenia* sp. in particular is very commonly seen in marine aquariums. Sometimes called "eye flukes" (although they live unseen on the fish's body just as well), this parasite will require proper treatment in order to save the fish.

This trematode is best eradicated using praziquantel administered in a quarantine tank at a rate of 0.20 ppm for seven days, followed by a 50% water change. After that, a second dose is administered followed by a second water change seven to ten days later.

Freshwater dips for five minutes will help diagnose this malady. After the dip, look at the bottom of the container for white, 1- to 2-mm oval shapes. These are dead flukes. Because *Neobenedenia* sp. is an egg-laying species, the flukes will still be present in the aquarium, even if the dip removed most of them from the fish.

ENVIRONMENTALLY INDUCED EYE PROBLEMS

Physical trauma

Exophthalmia can result from identifiable sources of trauma (such as the fish recently being captured and moved), but it is often from an unknown cause. The eye may or may not have clouding of the cornea, and bubbles may or may not be present.

A French angel with eye damage caused by a moray eel.

If this problem is suspected, the best treatment is to keep the fish safe from further trauma and see if it will resolve on its own. Aspirating the fluid or gas from behind the eye with a hypodermic needle is usually ineffective and may actually cause additional trauma through repeated handling of the fish.

Remember that capture trauma is one of the primary causes of exophthalmia, so capturing the affected fish time and time again to withdraw the gas or fluid is likely to only increase the damage. At the very least, it is imperative to use a sedative or anesthetic when attempting this sort of surgery, not only to reduce the fish's thrashing about, but also for humane consideration of the animal. For unknown reasons, mechanically induced exophthalmia is always restricted to marine fishes.

A lyretail anthias with severe bilateral exophthalmia; two surgeries did not resolve it, so the fish was humanely euthanized.

Some species of fish reported to be susceptible to mechanical exophthalmia:

Bigeyes	*Priacanthus* spp., *Pristigenys* spp.
Butterflyfish	*Chaetodon* spp.
Clownfish	*Amphiprion* spp.
Groupers	*Serranus* spp., *Anthias* spp., *Caesioperca* spp.
Hake	*Urophycis* spp.
Moorish Idol	*Zanclus cornutus*
Pinecone fish	*Monocentris japonica*
Rockfish	*Sebastes* spp.
Squirrelfish	*Holocentrus* spp., *Sargocentron* spp.
Scorpionfish	Most species, but less common with lionfish (*Pterois* spp.)
Whiptails	*Pentapodus* spp.
Wrasses	Labridae spp.

A *Sebastes* rockfish with bilateral retrobulbar exophthalmia; it healed with no treatment after a few months.

Sunken eye

This condition, known as enophthalmia, is the reverse of exophthalmia. In captive fishes, it is almost always caused by severe dehydration experienced by fish exposed to a sudden rise in the salinity of their water. In this case, the problem is always bilateral—affecting both eyes equally. Rarely, mechanical damage resulting in the puncture of the eye globe itself will result in the deflation, or enophthalmus, of just one eye.

Supersaturation

Typically, supersaturation (explained in detail in chapter 3) is caused by an air leak developing on the suction side of a pump or a sump pump that is allowed to "catch air," sometimes combined with water being pumped back into the aquarium without sufficient surface agitation.

There is no cure for this problem other than to rectify the cause of the supersaturation and offer the fish time to recover on its own. Public aquariums may have the ability to hold the fish in pressurized chambers or deep aquariums. This can recompress the gas and, if slowly depressurized, return the fish to normal condition.

Vitamin and dietary deficiencies

While deficiencies in certain vitamins have been reported to cause eye problems in fish (Hemdal 2006), in most of these cases, the problem can be demonstrated only in the laboratory when fish are fed diets completely lacking in certain nutrients. Aquarium fish that are being fed at least a relatively rounded diet will not show these extreme symptoms, and thus dietary causes of blindness are quite rare.

Riboflavin (vitamin B2) and vitamin A are both important for the continued eye health and proper vision in fishes. However, vitamin A is a fat-soluble vitamin and artificially high doses can be toxic to fish. Remember that supplementing these vitamins will not cure eye problems in fish that were initially caused by another factor. Two vitamins that sometimes are deficient in aquarium fish diets are thiamin (vitamin B12) and α-tocopherol (vitamin E), but these are not implicated in eye problems.

BLINDNESS

A very common symptom reported by home aquarists is that one of their fish has become blind. This, more often than not, is a result of a fish becoming ill to the point that it is moribund (close to death) and is not just blind. Basically, a fish that bumps around the aquarium, runs into the tank sides, and ignores food may not be blind at all; it may just be dying.

A truly blind fish will behave as if it is night and may even show its nighttime coloration. The fish will swim very cautiously to avoid running into obstacles, and it will orient itself in the normal upright position. If food is added to the tank, it will attempt to seek it out, perhaps by moving its mouth along the bottom of the tank, snapping up any food that it may come in contact with.

It is important for the aquarist to be able to distinguish the subtle differences between these two problems, as a truly blind fish may live for many years given extra care, while a moribund fish will continue its health decline and soon die if the problem is not corrected.

Bright aquarium lighting is sometimes implicated in causing blindness, especially in lionfish (*Pterois* spp.). Only anecdotal reports of this are available, and since aquarium lighting is many times less intense than on tropical reefs, cause and effect cannot be linked. Feeding freshwater fish to marine predators (again, often lionfish) is also reported by home aquarists to cause blindness. In these cases, it is most likely that the predator has developed fatty liver disease and the fish has become moribund from that.

A DIAGNOSTIC KEY TO FISH EYE PROBLEMS

The following key can be used by aquarists to evaluate problems they may have with their fish's eyes. To use this key, just answer each question and then proceed to the next question as directed. If you are unclear of any answers, try following the key through both branches and see if one result is a better fit for your fish's problem.

1. Assuming there is a group of fish in the aquarium, is more than one fish affected? If yes, go to #2; if no, go to #6. If the fish is being housed separately, you may need to explore both options to see which is a better fit.

2. Was the development of the eye problem rapid, involving many fish, typically with bilateral retrobulbar (behind the globe of the eye) exophthalmia and possibly air bubbles visible in some of their eyes? If yes, go to #4; if no, go to #3.

3. Are the corneas of most fish clear? If yes, go to #4; if corneas are cloudy, go to #5.

4. This may be a case of acute supersaturation of atmospheric gas in the fish's bloodstream.

5. Many fish in an aquarium exhibiting cloudy eyes typically is a sign of a widespread infection—see disease section.

6. With only one fish being affected, the problem is either just starting or it will be limited to that individual. Is the fish a Syngnathid (seahorse, pipefish, or seadragon)? If so, got to #7; otherwise go to #8.

7. Gas bubble disease (GBD) is a possibility.

8. If only one fish is affected, does it have exophthalmia in both eyes? If so, go to #10; if only in one eye, go to #9. If the fish does not exhibit exophthalmia, go to #11.

9. Commonly, exophthalmia that develops in one fish, in only one eye, is a result of physical trauma.
10. Mild bilateral exophthalmia in one fish can have many causes. Review the fish's history for possible infection-associated problems. In some cases, the cause cannot be determined; therefore, no treatment can be suggested.
11. Does the fish have the main symptom of not being able to see properly? If so, see the section on blindness; otherwise go to #12.
12. The remaining eye problems are typically chronic conditions, such as cataracts and droop-eye, for which there is no effective treatment.

A porcupinefish (*Diodon holocanthus*) with a cataract and gas bubbles in one eye.

KEEP AN EYE ON THOSE EYES!

Aquarists observing their fish will notice that the eye is a natural focal point. Look for changes in the eye, and then use the information in this section to predict a proper course of action.

But please remember that, although many observable problems with fish first show up as changes in their eyes, this is by no means always true. Therefore, examine the entire fish closely for any other subtle changes and analyze its overall demeanor—how well it is feeding, how it interacts with tankmates, its respiration rate, and whether it is alert and active overall. Aquarists who are highly alert to health changes in their fish are always better able to resolve the problem before fish loss occurs.

This stripey (*Microcanthus strigatus*) has chronic cataracts but has lived for years like this with no real difficulty.

TUMORS (NEOPLASMS)

As with mammals, fish can develop tumors (neoplasms) of various types. Some are benign while others are malignant and can spread throughout the fish. Tumors are generally only recognizable in fish if they are visible externally.

CAUSE

Some tumors, such as goiter, can be induced by environmental factors. In other cases, tumors develop as a result of viral infections (such as lymphocystis). Other potential predisposing factors include:

- Age: Older animals are more prone to developing neoplasms.
- Genetics: There is certainly a genetic predisposition to develop tumors in some individuals.
- Contaminated foods: Foods containing aflatoxins have been shown to cause liver tumors in fish.
- Repeated injury: Brushing against the aquarium wall, snout rubbing, and other repetitive injuries can cause granulomas.
- Other unidentified environmental causes.

SYMPTOMS

With few exceptions (e.g., flounders), fish are essentially bilateral creatures, and any deviation from how one side looks compared to the other indicates an abnormality. External tumors are easily identified as discolored growths on the skin of the fish. An internal tumor may be visible only as a slight lump. Unless the tumor is massive and involves internal organs, there are rarely any other symptoms that aquarists can see.

DIAGNOSIS

Positive diagnosis can really be made only by sending a biopsy out and having it examined by a pathologist.

TREATMENT

There is no home treatment for neoplasms in fish; surgery is the only option, and then only for non-malignant growths. Even these are likely to return after surgical removal. Supportive therapy, isolating the fish from more aggressive animals and keeping it under the best conditions possible, is the only other recommendation. Euthanasia may eventually be necessary.

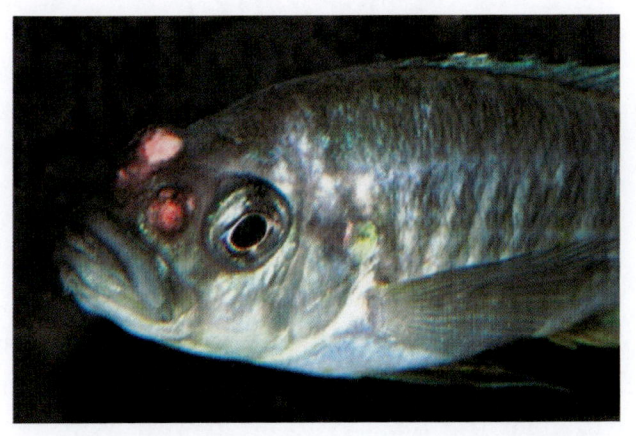

The lesions on this freshwater cichlid are probably neoplasms, but the damaged skin allows for secondary bacterial infection.

CHAPTER 5.
DISEASES OF INVERTEBRATES

Less is known about diseases of invertebrates than those of fishes, and that speaks volumes because so little is known about fish diseases to begin with. With respect to the diseases of marine invertebrates, two main factors need to be considered. First, many of these diseases can be controlled by giving the animal a proper environment. Second, newly acquired invertebrates need to be quarantined, as they can serve as disease vectors (carriers) for other invertebrates as well as fish that you already have in your aquarium.

INVERTEBRATES AS VECTORS FOR FISH DISEASES

One reason to properly quarantine newly acquired invertebrates is to reduce the possibility that their introduction may carry fish disease organisms into an aquarium.

It is well known that transferring small amounts of water from one aquarium to another can transfer disease organisms into the new tank. Pet dealers typically use strong disinfecting solutions (formalin or bleach) to reduce the chance of this happening when moving wet fish nets from one tank to another. Since there is a risk that fish diseases will adhere to the small volume of water on a wet fish net, it stands to reason that these same diseases can be transferred in any water moved from tank to tank, including water attached to invertebrate animals.

With invertebrates, however, the use of strong disinfectants is, of course, not possible. In these cases, the hope is that if the invertebrate (or live rock) is kept isolated from potentially affected fish longer than the parasites can survive without a fish host, the transfer can be made without introducing diseases to the fish. The problem is that this "clearing period" for fish parasites is not known with much certainty.

Some anecdotal information indicates that saltwater "ich" (*Cryptocaryon irritans*) can remain infective for at least 30 days without a host. The egg-laying trematode *Neobenedenia melleni* produces sticky eggs that may remain viable and potentially infective for more than 14 days.

If the invertebrate cannot be isolated from the general fish population for at least a month (the best-case scenario), other steps might help—e.g., rinsing the invertebrate with freshly mixed, sterile sea water may help to reduce the potential for disease introduction by physically washing away infective organisms.

DISEASES OF CRUSTACEANS

Some species of shrimp (notably the skunk cleaner shrimp, *Lysmata* sp.) arrive with epicaridean isopod infections that look like white lumps on the side of the shrimp's abdomen. Since the isopod is a crustacean itself, there is no treatment that will affect the parasite without killing the shrimp. Surgical removal is also not advised because crustaceans can only repair damage to their shells when they molt, so when the isopod is removed, a large wound will remain.

Many species of crustacean develop what is commonly known as "black spot shell disease." This is more of a symptom than a specific disease. Fungi, bacteria, algae, and protozoans can all grow on the shells of crustaceans, causing erosive damage that shows up as black spots. Because the shells of these animals only grow during the molting process, there is no treatment that will cure this problem between molts. Generally, if the animal molts frequently enough, the lesion will gradually heal on its own.

Black spot lesion on the shell of a giant Japanese spider crab.

DISEASES OF ECHINODERMS

Starfish and sea urchins may show signs of disease in captivity, such as dropped spines and open sores in sea urchins and loss of arms and open sores in starfish. Due to their sensitivity to medications, there is little one can do to resolve these problems other than provide the best possible environment.

Avoiding rapid changes in salinity, or lower-than-normal salinity, is very important with all starfish and sea urchins. For suspected bacterial diseases, an antibiotic dip, for one hour twice a day using an antibiotic effective against gram-negative bacteria, can be attempted (see formulary).

CORAL PESTS AND DISEASES

Corals, some other sessile invertebrates, and live rock have the potential to bring "hitchhikers" with them when they are transferred to a new aquarium. By far, the number-one scourge is an infestation of glass anemones (*Aiptasia* spp). Even one tiny anemone adhering to the base of a new coral can bring a plague of them into your display aquarium in a matter of months.

Other pests include various mantis shrimp and crabs that may arrive hiding inside live rock. Red bugs that attack *Acropora* corals, flatworms that eat corals of this same genus, and nudibranchs that feed on *Montipora* coral are all coral diseases that are frequently introduced with new animals.

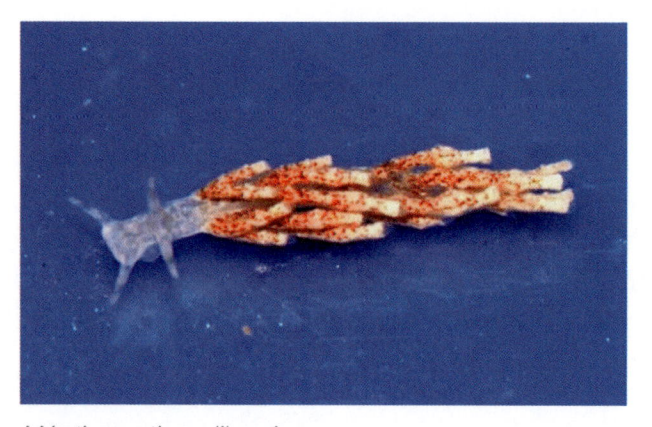

A *Montipora*-eating nudibranch.

Some argue that you can never completely eliminate the chance of introducing these pests, but many who believe this do not institute any sort of quarantine for their new invertebrates. Quarantine can and does help reduce the chance of introducing pests into your main aquarium.

The basic process is to have a small but completely furnished reef aquarium established where invertebrates (primarily corals) can be held in a pristine environment for at least eight weeks. This is also a perfect time to perform any light acclimation that your new corals may need.

After acclimation to the quarantine tank, place each new coral colony on a contrasting, smooth surface so that pests can more easily be seen. Egg crate, while good for anchoring coral "picks," is also a good place for coral pests to hide. A smooth, dark surface, such as PVC sheet, works well if the coral has a proper base that will allow it to sit upright.

An *Acropora* coral with flatworm eggs around its base. A small brittlestar is living on the dead white coral skeleton.

The colonies must be inspected for pests every few days and treated for problems accordingly. Obviously, this method takes time and effort and is most economical when done with a whole shipment of corals at the same time. But this process is good for weeding out serious pest issues that may be transferred on corals.

TREATMENTS

There are a variety of treatments for invertebrate problems, and they break down into three types: chemotherapy (dips and drugs added to the water), biological controls (adding other animals to control pests), and environmental maintenance (changing the aquarium's environment to favor one animal over another).

Chemotherapy

Chemotherapy is a difficult treatment method to use with invertebrates, as many of the pests you are trying to control have the same, or even less, sensitivity to a given drug than the corals do. Target applications can be used, such as topical chemical applications to control *Aiptasia* anemones. In other cases, dips have become very popular. Finally, there are systemic drugs, such as praziquantel, that are toxic to only certain groups of invertebrates.

For active quarantine systems, coral dips show the most promise. However, there are a variety of dips available. Some work for certain problems while others seem to show no real benefit. Heed the advice of your dealer or other people who have successfully used a given dip method. Avoid using any product that doesn't list its ingredients on the label. Would you take a prescription medication if your doctor refused to tell you what the active ingredient is?

Biological controls

Examples of biological control methods include using

copperband butterflyfish to control *Aiptasia* anemones, sixline wrasses to control flatworms, and various snails to control pest algae. These methods are best applied in instances where a pest has managed to enter your main reef aquarium, as they take time to work and rarely, if ever, completely eliminate a problem.

Environmental controls

Finally, there are environmental control methods. Many coral protozoan and bacterial diseases are ubiquitous—they are found in most aquariums—but only cause real problems when the corals are weakened by environmental problems. Improving the environment for the coral may allow it to become strong enough to rally and fight off the disease. In other cases, changing the environment by directing water flow can help mechanically brush off pests such as flatworms. Certainly, reducing dissolved wastes, such as nitrate and phosphate, can improve the coral's environment and help it fend off disease.

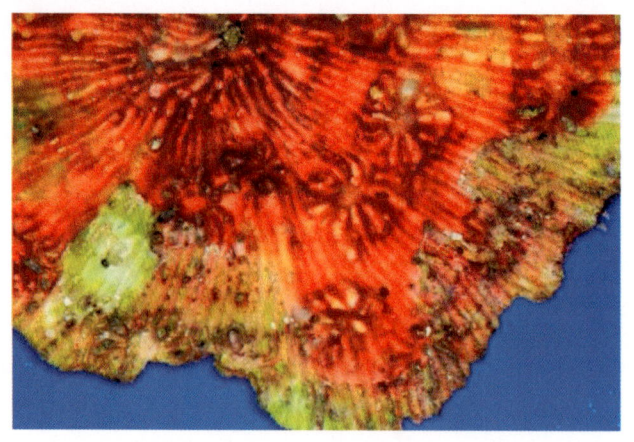

This pectiniid coral was stressed and damaged during shipping and handling—it did not recover.

In some cases, there simply is no truly effective treatment for a given problem (such as the protozoan infection known as brown jelly disease). Having these devastating problems show up in a quarantine tank is much preferred over seeing them rear their ugly head in your main reef tank. In these cases, you will need to leave the coral in quarantine, try to frag it, and remove the affected tissues—hoping the healthy frags will re-grow.

A *Montipora* coral with brown jelly disease caused by a protozoan.

CHAPTER 6.

EUTHANASIA

In this era of quick fixes and immediate gratification, it can be very difficult for hobbyists to accept the fact that some fish diseases are simply not going to respond to any medication or treatment thrown at them. Some ailing fishes, especially those with chronic diseases, simply cannot be cured and are slowly dying. At this point, euthanasia should be considered as a humane alternative to continued futile treatments.

DO FISH FEEL PAIN?

Some research has indicated that fish feel pain, while other studies show that they don't. The true answer probably lies somewhere in between; fish do feel an adverse stimulus, but it isn't "conscious pain" as seen in mammals. Whatever degree of pain or physical discomfort they experience, one could justifiably argue that allowing chronically ill fish to continue suffering is ethically questionable.

WHEN IS EUTHANASIA WARRANTED?

Euthanasia should be considered for a fish if 1) it has a chronic, untreatable disease (such as tumors, blindness, or starvation) or 2) the fish is "moribund" due to severe injury or illness. Moribund is a term that describes a fish that is still breathing but is unable to move on its own accord and obviously will not recover.

The American Veterinary Medical Association has their euthanasia guidelines posted online at http://bit.ly/avma-euthanasia-guidelines.

PREFERRED METHODS

MS-222

Every aquarist should have a plan for euthanasia before they need it. An overdose of buffered tricaine methanesulfonate (MS-222) is the preferred method for euthanizing fish. Dosing at a rate of greater than 300 mg/l MS-222 and 100 mg/l sodium bicarbonate is effective within 30 minutes.

Clove oil (eugenol)

One product that aquarists can buy that is approved by at least some veterinarians and research biologists is clove oil, also called eugenol. A dose of 50 mg/l is usually sufficient in euthanizing fish. This equates to about 0.20 ml of eugenol in one gallon of aquarium water.

Because eugenol does not mix well with water, and because larger volumes are easier for hobbyists to measure out, it can be dosed using the following method:

1. Add 2 ml of eugenol to 100 ml of tank water in a sealed container and shake it vigorously.
2. Add 10 ml of this suspended solution to each gallon of water needed to euthanize the fish.
3. Place the fish in this solution and keep it covered to prevent it from jumping out and to help keep it calm.
4. Wait at least ten minutes after it stops breathing, and then remove the fish from the solution and freeze it for later disposal.

OTHER METHODS

A variety of other methods have been proposed for home euthanasia of fishes, but none are fully accepted by veterinary medical experts. Still, home aquarists need some other tools to use, so the methods are listed here in roughly descending order of suitability:

ETHANOL

Regular alcohol at a dose of 25 ml per liter will cause respiratory collapse and death in fishes within 30 minutes. The trouble is that alcohol is not available in pure form unless it has been "denatured" by the addition of distasteful chemicals. Vodka is about 40% alcohol by volume, so using it at 62 ml per liter will give an effective dose.

DECAPITATION/PITHING

Cutting a fish's spinal cord, right behind the head, is a quick method of euthanasia that is approved for use in food fishes (where the use of chemicals would otherwise make the flesh unfit to eat). The issue is really that the method is distasteful for most people to do, so it is rarely used by hobbyists. However, it is quick and effective.

FREEZING

Placing the affected fish in a small amount of aquarium water in a sealed container and then placing the container in a freezer is a euthanasia technique used by some people. However, it is slow to work, so it is not considered humane. Its appeal as a method is that the fish is "out of sight" so people feel more detached from the process.

AN OPTION OF LAST RESORT

The animals in your aquariums are completely reliant on you for proper care. It is solely your responsibility to see to it that their lives in captivity are humane and that all of their needs are met. If you cannot meet their needs, please find someone who is more able. Euthanasia should be considered only for health reasons, not because it is no longer convenient to care for an animal.

CHAPTER 7.

ZOONOSIS AND DANGEROUS MARINE ORGANISMS

Note: While every attempt is made in this manual to give the reader the best possible advice for aquarium fish health problems, the author is not a medical doctor, so it is imperative that you consult with your physician promptly if you have any health concerns related to people and not fish.

ZOONOTIC DISEASE

While there are no reports of human diseases being transmitted to marine aquarium fish, marine fish can transmit diseases to people! A "zoonosis" or "zoonotic disease" is the medical term for a disease that can be transmitted from animals to humans. Some, like rabies, are very serious. For other zoonotic diseases, the seriousness of the infection is dependent upon the individual's level of health.

Aside from eating raw fish (which can transmit worm parasites to people), all of the zoonotic diseases that hobbyists need to be aware of are caused by bacteria. Groups known to be transmitted from marine aquariums to humans include *Pseudomonas*, *Staphylococcus*, *Vibrio*, and *Mycobacterium*.

The last one, *Mycobacterium*, tends to get the most "press." The other three typically cause skin infections similar to ones doctors see in non-aquarium cases, but *Mycobacterium* infection is stubborn to treat and causes a "false positive" in some human tuberculosis (TB) screening tests. Also called "swimming pool granuloma" and "fish handler's disease," atypical *Mycobacterium* can cause localized infections in the extremities of humans and, in some cases, results in a deep-seated infection that may require surgery. In other cases, the disease is self-limiting; it goes away on its own.

As an aquarium owner, if you ever test positive for human TB, you need to ask your physician to screen for atypical TB. Typically, serious cases of atypical *Mycobacterium* are seen only in people who have some other underlying health problem that makes them immune-compromised. The risk of infection from any aquarium bacterial zoonotic disease is minimal as long as a few safety precautions are taken.

PREVENTING HUMAN INFECTION

The following safety steps are intended to help prevent human infections from atypical "non-pulmonary" *Mycobacterium* spp. most commonly encountered in aquariums (*M. marinum, M. fortuitum,* and *M. chelonae*) as well as other potentially infectious bacteria:

1. Gloves should be worn by anyone working in aquariums, handling any seafood products, or performing a necropsy on an animal. Aquarists should wash their hands with a germicidal soap after removing gloves.

2. If shared for human food prep, all work surfaces and kitchen equipment should be decontaminated after each use. A 10% solution of household bleach in water (5000 ppm sodium hypochlorite) is an effective disinfectant.

3. Never siphon aquarium water by mouth—the risk of ingesting contaminated water is too great. Start siphons by filling the hose with tap water first.

4. Foods for human consumption should be stored separate from frozen or fresh aquarium seafoods.

5. Immune-compromised persons should be especially careful around aquariums, as they are more

susceptible to infection and more likely to exhibit serious complications if they do become infected.

DANGEROUS MARINE ANIMALS AND PLANTS

Most aquarists are aware that some species of aquarium animals can directly harm humans. Lionfish are known to have a venomous sting, and moray eels can bite, of course, but there are lesser-known dangers that could be lurking in your home aquarium. Here are some examples:

BLUE-RING OCTOPUS

A bite from a blue-ring octopus (*Hapalochlaena* spp.) can be lethal. What's more, they make poor display animals and no antivenin is available. Avoid contact with this species, and keep the aquarium tightly covered. The toxin of this species has been identified as being identical to tetrodotoxin—the same as in certain puffers, which has no known antidote. There may be other species of octopus that also possess a dangerous bite, so take care when handling any species.

CAULERPA

This decorative algae is reported to contain toxic compounds. For humans, this would be a concern only if somebody tried to eat it.

Never ingest *Caulerpa* algae.

CONE SHELLS

These attractive snails have a long dart, known as a radula, that they use to inject venom. Some species are dangerous to humans, and many look alike, so it is best to handle any cone shell with tongs instead of by hand.

FIRE ANEMONE (*ACTINODENDRON PLUMOSUM*)

All anemones can sting, but they rarely cause severe problems. In certain people, repeated contact with anemones results in a sensitivity reaction. To avoid developing this syndrome, you may wish to use rubber gloves when handling these animals. The fire anemone (also called the hellfire anemone) can give a severe sting. Even nets that touch this anemone can transfer nematocysts that can then sting a person.

FIREWORMS

These reddish-brown annelid worms commonly live in aquarium gravel. They are covered with silicate spicules that can break off in skin. Contact with them results in a mild form of dermatitis. Prevention is a simple matter of wearing gloves when handling live rock or aquarium gravel.

PALYTOXIN

Produced by some soft corals, this is one of the most toxic marine compounds yet discovered. Palytoxin is not found in all soft corals, and much still needs to be learned about it. There is some speculation that the toxin is not produced by the coral itself, but by a dinoflagellate growing in the coral tissue. Aquarists have reported serious reactions from handling soft corals. Not all of these reported reactions may have been due to palytoxin; some may have been allergic reactions and others a result of aquarium bacteria entering a wound. Regardless of the actual cause, aquarists are reminded to handle corals only when wearing latex gloves. When fragmenting corals, one should most certainly wear eye protection and a respirator. Keep soft corals out of reach of children and pets.

This watermelon zoanthid may contain palytoxin.

SCORPIONFISH, LIONFISH, RABBITFISH

Many fish have venomous spines along their dorsal fins, pelvic fins, gill covers, or anal fins. The toxicity of the venom varies from species to species and person to person. First aid for these wounds is mainly to submerge the injury in water that is as hot as the person can stand and get medical attention.

Treat all scorpionfish, such as this lionfish, with caution.

SPONGES

Some species can cause dermatitis in humans when touched. The red beard sponge (*Microciona* sp.) and the fire sponge (*Tedonia* sp.) are the worst of these. To be safe, treat any red or brown sponge with caution.

STINGRAYS AND CATFISH

These can inject venom through sharp spines (on the tail for rays, on the dorsal and pectoral fins for catfish). First aid is the same as for lionfish. Two species of catfish, the striped sea catfish (*Plotosus* sp.) and the sea catfish (*Arius* sp.), are highly toxic. Most injuries from these fish occur when they are stuck in a net and the person is attempting to remove them. There is no antivenin for the stings of either of these types of fish.

Until otherwise informed, consider any new aquatic animal you are unfamiliar with to be potentially dangerous!

CHAPTER 8.

FISH PHARMACOLOGY AND FORMULARY

Much of the information about aquarium medicine is anecdotal, based on various personal experiences. Human medicine differs in that there is much more support in terms of clinical drug trials and available scientific literature. This section attempts to familiarize aquarists with standard medical techniques and terminology so they can extrapolate veterinary and human medicine information more accurately and efficiently.

The obvious difficulty is that over-extrapolation of information has long been a problem for aquarists. Techniques suitable for humans do not always translate into an effective treatment strategy for fishes. Still, if all one has is anecdotal information of unknown quality, borrowing from another medical field may be a better starting point.

METHODS OF ADMINISTERING CHEMOTHERAPEUTICS

Almost all routes of drug administration in animals and humans can be used in fishes. The decision of which route to choose is based on the ability to restrain or capture the animal, the form of the drug available, and how quickly the drug's effect is needed.

EXTERNAL APPLICATIONS

When drugs are administered externally to fish, the contact time is very important. Too short of a time and the drug will not be effective; too long and the fish may be damaged by exposure to the drug or removal from the water.

TOPICAL TREATMENTS

The technique of painting a medication on the skin of a fish has been used for many years. Care must be taken in choosing the drug, as some medications for terrestrial animals may be toxic if absorbed through a fish's skin, and the drug may be harmful if it washes off into the aquarium's water when the fish is returned to the tank.

For topical treatments, the fish is removed from the water and a concentrated form of the medication is applied to the infection site. Contact time may need to be as great as ten minutes. In some cases, the fish can be restrained with its gills submerged to allow it to breathe, but in other cases, an anesthetic may be required.

DIPS

Other medications or treatments are administered through a more diluted concentration, but for a slightly longer time. "Dips" typically consist of placing the fish in water combined with some medication for anywhere from 3 minutes to an hour. Formalin is commonly used as a dip medication.

The dosage is variable between time and concentration: low concentration/long dip time and high concentration/shorter dip time. The water volume used for a dip is generally just enough to support the animal comfortably during the process, so the amount of medication used is kept to a minimum. If the planned dip will take longer than 10 minutes, supplemental aeration may be required.

STATIC BATHS

A static bath is the same as a dip except that the treatment time is longer and the drug concentration is more dilute. Bath treatment times can range from 4 hours to days or even weeks at a time. They are normally performed on fish that have an effective life-support system in order to maintain water quality. Although the drug concentration is lower in a static bath, the volume of water is much greater than in a dip, so this form of treatment can become very expensive.

A major benefit of this type of treatment is that various

life stages of the disease organism can be targeted and the life cycle can be more easily disrupted. Take, for example, an instance where a formalin dip is performed to remove trematodes from the skin of a fish but then the fish is re-infected when it is returned to its aquarium and new trematode eggs hatch out. In that same situation, a long-term praziquantel bath performed in the aquarium itself would effectively kill the trematodes as well as all the larvae as they hatch from their eggs.

ORAL (PER OS, PO)

Orally dosed medications are very cost-effective because only the fish is dosed, not all of the water in the aquarium. The obvious drawback is that the fish to be treated must still be healthy enough to be feeding normally. Another, less obvious problem is that most oral medications are dosed based on the specimen's weight; unless the fish can be captured and weighed, its weight must be estimated. Oral medications can also be administered by force, through tube-feeding.

INJECTION

Drugs that are given by injection are called parenteral drugs. The three routes used for fish are intramuscular (IM), intravascular (IV), and intraperitoneal (IP). Care must be taken when injecting antibiotics so that a sterile abscess is not created. Careful choice of the drug and using a dilution factor that minimizes the volume to be injected both may help reduce this problem. IP injections are normally avoided because there is too much danger of inadvertently injecting the drug directly into a major organ, such as the liver.

FREQUENCY OF ADMINISTRATION

Medical terminology is used when describing the frequency of delivery of a drug:

- Once a day—SID, every 24 hours
- Twice a day—BID, every 12 hours
- Three times daily—TID, every 8 hours
- Four times daily—QID, every 6 hours
- Every other day—EOD, once every 48 hours
- Every third day—ETD, once every 72 hours

DRUG TYPES

Because aquarium drugs are derived from human and veterinary medicine, the variety available is huge and growing larger all the time. The choice of which medication to use is difficult and must take into account the status of the animal's disease (morbidity), environmental factors (e.g., tetracycline is often inactivated by calcium in sea water), effectiveness at controlling the target disease, toxicity to the fish (or side effects), cost, delivery method required for use, and potential resistance of the disease organism.

The following classes of drugs are used in aquariums:

- Antibacterial
- Antifungal
- Antiparasitic

- Anesthetic
- Hormones and steroids
- Nutritional and mineral supplements
- Fluid support

Very few drugs are FDA approved for use in fishes, and fewer still are allowable for use in food fishes. This "off-label" use is allowed if administered under the direction of a veterinarian. Many of these same drugs are commonly sold in pet stores, but the legality of this is being questioned.

Follow a few safety steps at all times:

- Discard all outdated medication.
- Keep all aquarium chemicals out of the reach of children.
- Do not repeat antibiotic therapies indiscriminately (to avoid the development of resistant strains of bacteria).
- Keep all drugs in their original, labeled containers.
- Avoid using chloramphenicol, as it can cause aplastic anemia in some people.

FORMULARY

COPPER SULFATE STOCK SOLUTION

Dissolve 13.6 grams of $CuSO_4$ or 21.3 grams of $CuSO_4 \times 5\ H_2O$ into 1000 ml of distilled water. Add 9.1 grams of citric acid. Store in dark glass or plastic bottle.

Calculating dosage:

The target concentration of ionic copper is usually 0.20 ppm. 1 ml of the stock solution will treat 7 gallons of water at that level.

Treating the tank:

Twice a day, the tank is tested with a copper test kit. The Hach Porphyrin method seems to give the most accurate results. Simply re-dose the copper stock solution in accordance with the current copper reading: a reading of .15 ppm indicates that a 1/4 dose should be added, etc.

COPPER—ORGANICALLY CHELATED PROPRIETARY SOLUTIONS

These are typically less toxic to fish but may take longer to effect a cure than copper sulfate solutions. Follow label directions.

FORMALITE STOCK SOLUTION

For a 300 ml stock solution, add 224 ml of formalin to 75.7 ml distilled water. To this, dissolve 2.25 grams of malachite green. 7.6 ml of this solution will treat 100 gallons of water at full strength.

Calculating the dosage:

For full strength treatment, add 7.6 ml of the stock solution per 100 gallons of actual tank capacity. A "low dose" is used with some species that might not survive a full dose. In this case, use 5 ml of the stock solution. For very sensitive fish, use at half strength, or 3.8 ml per 100 gallons. Dose formalite every 48 hours for 3 to 5 treatments. Change 50% of the tank water just prior to the treatments.

Warnings:

Never use formalite in tanks containing fish for human consumption. Always remove carbon and other chemical filtration from the tank prior to the treatment. Always test a given species for possible sensitivity before treating a large number of them. Never use formalite in tanks containing live plants or invertebrates. Formalite has proven toxic to elephantnose fish, characins, as well as some scaleless fishes.

AMIKACIN

Use – systemic bacterial disease.
Dose – 2.7 mg per .9 kg of fish weight, injected IM for three treatments spaced 48 hours apart.
Notes – It is difficult to inject small fishes.

CHLOROQUINE HCL

Use – external anti-protozoan, anti-metazoan. May also have antibiotic effects and will kill *Aiptasia* anemones.
Dose – 8 to 15 ppm as a static bath.
Notes – Will usually inhibit nitrifying bacteria, so ammonia levels must be monitored after treatment. Some fish have shown sensitivity to doses above 10 ppm (lionfish and wrasses).

CIPROFLOXACIN

Use – external bacterial diseases of marine fishes.
Dose – 7.5 ppm as a static bath, 150 ppm as a 1-hour dip.

KANAMYCIN

Use – antibiotic for external bacterial diseases of fishes.
Dose – 750 mg/l for a 2-hour bath.

LUGOL'S SOLUTION

Use – dip or swab as an antibiotic for corals or injuries on fish.
Dose – full dose as a 20-second swab, then rinse with sea water and return to the aquarium.
Notes – This product contains elemental iodine and is toxic to humans. Its sale and use may be restricted in some areas.

NEOMYCIN SULFATE

Use – external for gram-negative bacterial diseases.
Dose – 25 mg per gallon as a static bath.

NITROFURAZONE

Use – external for gram-positive and gram-negative bacteria.
Dose – 25 mg per gallon as a static bath.

PRAZIQUANTEL

Use – oral medication for some helminthes.
Dose – 238 mg active drug per 100 g of food daily for 3 to 5 days.
Notes – Can be used as an external dip at 10 ppm for 3 hours every other day for 3 to 5 treatments. Static bath is the most popular treatment method; dose at 2.2 mg/l up to 4 mg/l in stubborn cases. Disperse praziquantel into the water by pressing it through a nylon stocking.

MEDICATION DOSE CALCULATION

Dosing medications in the United States is confounded by the fact that we tend to measure medications using metric units but tank volume is measured in gallons. The basic equation for calculating these medication dosages is as follows: Parts per million projected dose times net gallons of water divided by 266 equals grams or milliliters of medication to be added.

X ppm x Y gallons / 266 = Z grams of medication
(Since a milliliter of most liquids weighs one gram, volume can often be used interchangeably.)

Sample: You need to dose a tank that holds 25 gallons of water with formalin at 75 parts per million. How much do you add?
25 x 75 = 1875
1875 ÷ 266 = 7.05

Rounding this value off, you should add 7.1 milliliters of formalin to the tank to achieve the desired dose of formalin.

TANK VOLUME CALCULATIONS

For a rectangular aquarium, length x width x height (in inches) divided by 231 will give you the base gallon capacity of the tank.

To refine this base capacity:

Measure the inside of the tank from the average surface of the gravel to the waterline for the height measurement described above. Then calculate the volume of your gravel bed. To do this, multiply the depth of the gravel by the width and length of the aquarium. Divide this by 231. Finally, divide this result by 3. This will give an approximate volume of the water contained between the grains of gravel in your filter bed. Add this value to your base gallon capacity.

Next, you need to subtract water displaced by any tank decorations, live rock, etc. There is no easy way to do this. For a standard "fish aquarium" decorated with a few pieces of coral, the amount to be subtracted is usually around 15%.

Finally, attempt to calculate the volume of water held in the sump, if applicable.

Of course, the best way to determine the volume of a given tank is to count the number of gallons it takes to fill it for the first time.

CLOSING THOUGHT

With a little effort and some guidance on how to direct that effort, you can increase the survivability of the fish in your marine aquarium by a huge factor. This, in turn, means you'll buy fewer replacement fish, saving you money and making the hobby itself more environmentally sustainable.

The information contained in this book is a compilation of my 45-plus years of experience working in public aquariums and the pet industry and keeping home aquariums. I truly want to see every marine aquarist achieve success, but the information provided here is only a start; you must then take the initiative to apply it—and even look for ways to improve upon it.

ABOUT THE AUTHOR

Jay Hemdal has been an avid marine aquarist for over 45 years and set up his first marine aquarium when he was nine years old. He worked part time for many years at various local retail pet stores and fish wholesale companies while he was living at home and later at college. After graduating from college, he managed the aquarium department of a large retail pet store for five years until 1985, when he was hired as an aquarist/diver (and later department manager) for the John G. Shedd Aquarium in Chicago. In 1989, he accepted the position of curator of fishes and invertebrates for the Toledo Zoo, where he still works today. Jay has written over 150 magazine articles and six previous books since 1981.

ABOUT THE PUBLISHER

Saltwater Smarts is a unique online resource created by long-time aquarists Chris Aldrich and Jeff Kurtz to inspire and entertain a new generation of marine aquarium hobbyists while helping them acquire the reliable, authoritative knowledge base they need to succeed with a saltwater system. By clarifying key concepts, techniques, and terminology, as well as sharing expert insights from fellow enthusiasts and industry professionals, Chris and Jeff hope to promote a more accessible, sustainable, and enjoyable marine aquarium hobby.

Your head start to marine aquarium success

WWW.SALTWATERSMARTS.COM

REFERENCES

Hemdal, J.F. 2014. "Viral Diseases of Aquarium Fishes," *TFH* Magazine.

Hemdal, J.F. Odum, R.A. 2011. "The Role of Activated Lignite Carbon in the Development of Head and Lateral Line Erosion in the Ocean Surgeonfish." North American Journal of Aquaculture 73:4, 489-492.

Hemdal, J.F. 2013. "Chloroquine: A 'New' Drug for Treating Fish Diseases." Advanced Aquarist's Online Magazine. 12(2): http://bit.ly/1viZi1n.

——2010. "The 'Eyes' Have it: A Review of Eye Health in Aquarium Fishes." Advanced Aquarist's Online Magazine. 9(3): http://bit.ly/1xUGsQg.

——2010. "Red Band Syndrome." Aquarium Fish International 22(1):26-30.

——2009. "Mortality Rates of Fishes in Captivity." Advanced Aquarist's Online Magazine. 8(12): http://bit.ly/1FkuWgl.

——2008. *Mini-Aquariums*. 144p. BowTie Press, Laguna Hills, California.

——2007. "Chronic Anorexia in Aquarium Fishes." Advanced Aquarist's Online Magazine. 6(12): http://bit.ly/11QJo3d.

–2006. *Advanced Marine Aquarium Techniques*. 352pp. TFH Publications, Neptune City, New Jersey.

Shors, Teri (2008). *Understanding Viruses*. Jones and Bartlett Publishers.

Sriwanayos P, Francis-Floyd R, Stidworthy MF, Petty BD, Kelley K, Waltzek TB. 2013 "Megalocytivirus infection in orbiculate batfish Platax orbicularis." Diseases of Aquatic Organisms. 105(1):1-8.

Varner, Patricia W. & Donald H. Lewis. 1991. "Characterization of a Virus Associated with Head and Lateral Line Erosion Syndrome in Marine Angelfish." Journal of Aquatic Animal Health 3:198-205.

Weber ES 3rd, Waltzek TB, Young DA, Twitchell EL, Gates AE, Vagelli A, Risatti GR, Hedrick RP, Frasca S Jr. 2009. "Systemic iridovirus infection in the Banggai cardinalfish (*Pterapogon kauderni* Koumans 1933)." Journal of Veterinary Diagnostic Investigation.

Wolf, K. 1988. *Fish Viruses and Fish Viral Diseases*. Cornell University Press.

Printed in Great Britain
by Amazon